# 69 Simple Science Fair Projects With Model Rockets: *Aeronautics*

*By Timothy S. Van Milligan*

COMPONENTS

Colorado Springs, Colorado

69 Simple Science Fair Projects with Model Rockets: Aeronautics
©1996 Timothy S. Van Milligan. All Rights Reserved.
Second Printing, 1999.

Cover Artwork by: Darby Perrin Aviation Art, Midwest City, Oklahoma.

ISBN 0-9653620-0-0

Published by:  Apogee Components, Inc.
1431 Territory Trail,
Colorado Springs, Colorado, 80919-3323
USA

*Dedicated to Patrick McCarthy, who in 1983 showed me all the great things that make rocketry such an enjoyable hobby.*

# Preface

# Why you should read this book!

So you want to do a science fair project? You saw this book and you thought that it would be neat to combine something interesting like model rocketry with your science fair project. Well, I would like to be the first to congratulate you on making a very great choice! Model rocketry offers a very wide selection of topics that can be explored, but the *best* reason to choose model rocketry is that it is a lot of fun! By choosing something that is fun, you are going to be more interested in the project, and you will have less of a tendency to put it off to the very last minute. You'll also have more motivation to do more work, because after all, it's not really work, it's a fun activity!

You probably picked up this book because you needed a topic to do your research. This book will definitely help you in that area, and much more. Besides listing a great variety of topics, this book will also give you help on where to start the project. More importantly, it will give you some very good hints on how to obtain valuable data from your experiment. After all, if you can't prove your hypothesis or make a concluding statement based on your collected data, you probably won't have a desire to write up a good final report to go with the science fair project.

The other type of person that may pick up this book is the classroom teacher. You may be teaching about the subject of model rocketry, and after building and flying a basic model rocket, you will probably have a desire to use model rockets to do more. The fascination of students for model rocketry makes it a great tool to use to further develop their desire to learn. This book will help in those situations too, because the same topics used for science fair projects also make great classroom projects!

Whatever your reason, this book will give you a great starting point. This book describes 69 different science fair experiments using model rockets that explore various principles of aeronautics. These projects are designed to be "simple to understand" and "easy to perform," so that even young students can participate in this fun and educational activity.

This book is more than just a listing of projects — each experiment also contains basic background information about the topic, so the student understands the topics, and why it is needed to be researched. Helpful ideas and hints on how the project should be set up and where the student can get more information are also listed for each project.

Because gathering the data is so important to these projects, a special section on tracking methods and data gathering techniques is presented near the beginning of this book. Even though you might think it is a major chore to gather flight information, you will be surprised at how easy it is to get great data from each launch.

## Why this book reads like an advertisement

As you read through this book, you'll soon discover that I *strongly* and *repeatedly* endorse the products from Apogee Components. I apologizes to anyone who is offended by the book being an advertisement. But there are two good reasons for my endorsement of Apogee's products; first: I liked the products so much that I bought the company. Second, many of the publications and products from Apogee Components were developed by your author, and are the best source of information on the subject of model rocketry. If there was something better (which was also easily accessible), I would let you know.

But even though the book is a lengthy advertisement, I am positive that you will find what you are looking for. You picked this book up because you wanted a topic that could be researched with model rocketry; and I won't disappoint you. There are 69 major projects listed in this book, as well as many "small projects" that are sub-parts of the major ones. When you add to this the number of new ideas that you will generate, you will be happy that you bought this book.

When you do a great exhibit that started from ideas generated as a result of reading this book, I'll feel that I have accomplished my goal — *"to make rocketry more than just fun; to show the educational benefits as well."*

Timothy S. Van Milligan
Spring, 1996

# Table of Contents

# Chapter 1

# Rocketry Safety

*MPORTANT! DON'T SKIP THIS SECTION!*

Safety is the most important thing that you should concern yourself with when building and launching any model rocket. Although the nature of scientific investigations is to push the limits of performance, you should never overlook the safety aspects.

To keep the hobby of rocketry safe, a special code of conduct has been created to give you guidance. Follow these rules, because they have been thoughtfully devised to keep you and others from getting hurt.

Here is the National Association's Model Rocket Safety Code. Read it, understand it, and commit yourself to following it. You might also include a copy of it in your final report to show the judges of your science fair that you have concern with this aspect of rocketry.

### National Association of Rocketry's Safety Code

1. *Materials*: My model rocket will be made of lightweight materials such as paper, wood, rubber, and plastic suitable for the power used and the performance of my model rocket. I will not use any metal for the nose cone, body, or fins of a model rocket.
2. *Engines*: I will use only commercially-made NAR certified model rocket engines in the manner recommended by the manufacturer. I will not alter the model rocket engine, it parts, or its ingredients in any way.
3. *Recovery*: I will always use a recovery system in my rocket that will return it safely to the ground so it may be flown again. I will use only flame-resistant recovery wadding if required.
4. *Weight Limits*: My model rocket will weigh no more that 1500 grams (53 oz.) at lift-off, and its rocket engines will produce no more than 320 Newton-seconds of total impulse. My model rocket will weigh no more than the engine manufacturer's recommended maximum lift-off weight for the engines used, or I will use engines recommended by the manufacturer for my model rocket.

**5.** *Stability*: I will check the stability of my model rocket before its first flight, except when launching a model rocket of already proven stability.

**6.** *Payloads*: Except for insects, my model rocket will never carry live animals or a payload that is intended to be flammable, explosive, or harmful.

**7.** *Launch Site*: I will launch my model rockets outdoors in a cleared area, free of tall trees, power lines, buildings, and dry brush and grass. I will ensure that people in the launch area are aware of the pending model rocket launch and can see the model rocket's liftoff before I begin my audible five-second countdown.

**8.** *Launcher*: I will launch my model rocket from a stable launching device that provides rigid guidance until the model rocket has reached a speed adequate to ensure a safe flight path. To prevent accidental eye injury, I will always place the launcher so that the end of the rod is above eye level or I will cap or dissassemble my launch rod when not in use and I will never store it in an upright position. My launcher will have a jet deflector device to prevent the engine exhaust from hitting the ground directly. I will always clear the area around my launch device of brown grass, dry weeds, or other easy-to-burn materials.

**9.** *Ignition System*: The system I use to launch my model rocket will be remotely controlled and electrically operated. It will contain a launching switch that will return to "off" when released. The system will contain a removable safety interlock in series with the launch switch. All persons will remain at least 5 meters (15 feet) from the model rocket when I am igniting the model rocket engines totalling 30 Newton-seconds or less of total impulse and at least 9 meters (30 feet) from the model rocket when I am igniting model rocket engines totaling more than 30 Newton-seconds of total impulse. I will use only electrical igniters recommended by the engine manufacturer that will ignite model rocket engine(s) within one second of actuation of the launching switch.

**10.** *Launch Safety*: I will not allow anyone to approach a model rocket on a launcher until I have made certain that the safety interlock has been removed or that the battery has been disconnected from the ignition system. In the event of a misfire, I will wait one minute after a misfire before allowing anyone to approach the launcher.

**11.** *Flying Conditions*: I will launch my model rocket only when the wind is less than 30 kilometers (20 miles) an hour. I will not launch my model rocket so it flies into clouds, near aircraft in flight, or in a manner that is hazardous to people or property.

**12.** *Pre-Launch Test*: When conducting research activities with unproven model rocket designs or methods I will, when possible, determine the reliability of my model rocket by prelaunch tests. I will conduct the launching of an unproven design in complete isolation from persons not participating in the actual launching.

**13.** *Launch Angle*: My launch device will be pointed within 30 degrees from vertical. I will never use model rocket engines to propel any device horizontally.

**14.** *Recovery Hazards*: If a model rocket becomes entangled in a power line or other dangerous place, I will not attempt to retrieve it.

This is the official Model Rocket Safety Code of the National Association of Rocketry. Note: The largest "model" rocket engine defined by the CPSC is an "F" (80 N-s). To launch rockets weighing over 1.36 Kg (3 pounds) including motor propellant, or rockets motors containing more than 62.5 grams (2.2 ounces) of propellant, you must obtain a waiver from the Federal Aviation Administration (FAA). Check your telephone directory for the FAA office nearest you. They will be able to help, and you must obtain their permission to operate rockets larger than those listed above.

# Chapter 2

# Science Fair Projects Basics

## Overview of Science Fair Projects

The *science fair* is an exhibition at which students may present projects that include an experiment they have performed. A project may be the work of an individual student or a group of students and includes the following components:

A. An experiment that follows the scientific method.
B. Research.
C. A laboratory report or log.
D. An abstract.
E. A display board.
F. An oral presentation.

## Selecting a Topic

Selecting a topic is a difficult task. Obtain a list of allowable categories from your science teacher to help focus on the area of science you wish to investigate. Aviation and rocketry are allowable subject areas to research; but these are often broken down into more specific categories that might include area of study such as propulsion systems, and flight control systems. Choose a category you are interested in and would like to learn more about. Besides the ideas listed in this book, you can also talk to your teachers, parents, librarians, classmates and members of the community for ideas. Also look through science books and magazines or visit museums for ideas. Once you have selected a topic, determine the availability of materials necessary to conduct your experiment. If you cannot obtain all of the materials, you may need to do some re-thinking about what to perform.

## Safety

Safety is a concern for all rocketry science projects and a reputation for which, the National Association of Rocketry proudly enjoys. If you haven't already done so, go back and read the previous chapter in this book. Obvious concerns are that your project conform to your school's lab safety standards. Hazardous materials should not be openly displayed. This may include combustible solids, liquids or gases which would exclude examples of your model rocket engines. However, there is NO danger in displaying used engine casings. As stated in the NAR Safety Code, NO live vertebrate animals should be used in your experiment. Even when using insects in a project, they should be used in a humane manner. Results of your research should be shown on graphs, charts, photographs or video, not the actual insects themselves.

### Get Organized

Planning is the key phase to a successful project. Don't leave things until the last minute. To help you get going, start a *Project Log*. This is just an informal record to keep tracked of how you are coming along on the project. This log should include the following:

a) Your hypothesis (what the experiment will attempt to prove).
b) How the experiment will be performed, including set-up, testing and observations that need to be taken.
c) Research that needs to be completed.
d) Supplies to be purchased.
e) Items you will construct on your own.
f) Analyzing the data collected.
g) Preparing the final report.
h) Constructing the display.

Starting the actual project begins with research. Don't fool yourself; research is a big part of your experiment. Many people hate doing this step and wonder why it is required. There are many reasons why research needs to be done. First, the results of your research will help you develop your hypothesis and help narrow the focus of your project. By researching your topic, you will know what was done in the past, and this may save you the time and effort of trying to prove an idea that is already proven "fact."

Similarly, it will show you what not to do - you don't want to repeat a failed experiment, unless you know where others have gone wrong and have a new way to perform the experiment.

There are many resources where you can obtain information about your topic, the library is just one—but a great place to start. Books, magazines and newspapers are a major resource. Video tapes and television offer many science related shows. Government agencies, community members involved in science and local businesses may provide additional information and materials. If these don't help you, check the list of other sources of information at the end of this booklet. The National Association of Rocketry (NAR) in Altoona, Wisconsin, is a major source for model rocketry related information and materials.

During your research, make sure to take accurate and adequate notes. Having more than you need is better than not having enough. Make sure you understand what you read and write. This may necessitate further research and may lead you to areas for future exploration which can be included in your report's conclusion. Make sure to use your own words when writing the research section of your lab report. Keep a record of where you got your information. This information will become the bibliography of the final report that you write.

### The Scientific Method — The Starting Point of all Experiments

When performing any science fair project, you will want to follow the scientific method. The scientific method contains and employs specific steps :

| | |
|---|---|
| **The Problem** | Stated in the form of a question. The "problem" is the idea you wish to investigate. |
| **The Hypothesis** | A possible answer to your problem based on your research and experience. |
| **The Procedure** | A description of the experiment. |
| **The Results** | The data and observations collected during the experiment. |
| **The Conclusion** | A statement that answers the problem based on your interpretation of the data and observations. |

Following the scientific method insures the continuity of scientific experimentation. It allows for reproducibility of the experiment and results, and to obtain proof of the hypothesis. Proving hypotheses leads to formulation of theories.

### The Proposal / Hypothesis

The hypothesis is a concise statement as to what you expect to prove with your experiment. Such a hypothesis might be: *"I expect a rocket with streamlined fins to fly higher than a rocket with fins that have blunt edges."* Many people have found it is hard to come up with a topic and a hypothesis to go along with it. This book will help you if you have this problem. It lists many topics that can be studied with model rockets.

## Developing Your Project

In your logbook, state your experiment's objective, which is a restatement of the hypothesis. Jot down how you think the rocket will perform, and how the performance will change if you change a variable.

From these notes, you will begin to develop your experiment and procedures. As you perform this task, you need to keep in mind that it must be a controlled experiment. You will want to make sure that you launch your models with as little variation as possible. For example, if you launch on two different days, the weather conditions on those two days should be as similar as possible. If it is calm on one day, and really windy the next, this could change the results of the experiment.

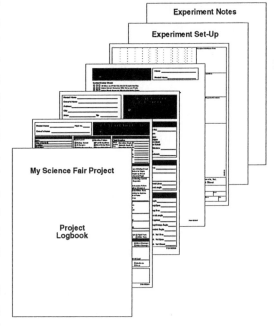

Weather is just one variable (or parameter) that you should attempt to maintain constant from one launch to the next. All the variables, except one, should be kept the same between each launch.

How do you know which variable changed? First you must define a starting point, which will be your *control* rocket. You will make your conclusions by showing how different models perfom against the control model. For example, if you are testing the shapes of different nose cones, first test your control rocket and determine how it flies, such as how high, how straight, or how long it takes it to go from liftoff to apogee. Then if you switch to a different shape nose cone, you will determine if it performed better or worse compared to the control model.

It is important that you change only one variable at a time. If you change both the nose cone and the shape of the fins, you won't know which item caused the change in performance when compared to the control model.

Another important variable that is often overlooked in many experiments is the mass of the model. This is particularly critical in any project where you are going to compare the altitude or duration in the air of two or more launches. If one model weighs more than the other, it will affect the height achieved. The easiest way to make sure your rockets weigh the same is to add weight to the lighter one; this is a lot easier to do than to try and remove weight from the heavier one. The easiest substance to use is tracking powder, such as Tempra paint or ground chalk. It can be added just prior to placing the model on the launch pad, and it will help you see the model in the sky when the parachute is deployed.

Your project log should keep an accurate description of the control rocket, so that you know what was changed between each flight. You may find that the *"Apogee Rocket Data Sheet"* from Apogee Components is a useful form to define and document information about the basic rocket configuration. This form lists the important parameters of the rocket, such as size, weight, fin shape, type and size of recovery device, etc.

A similar data sheet can also be filled out for each model where you changed something. In this way, you will always know which variable was changed, and you will be able to compare it to the control model.

## Collecting and recording Data

Use a notebook to record all your measurements and observations. Record data immediately, do not expect to memorize and then be able to record it later. You'll forget too much data.

Determine the units of measurement beforehand. Use of the Metric system is highly recommended. When making observations, note the date and time. Consider taking photographs or video tape for use in your report or as part of the display. If you are personally conducting a part of the experiment, such as a model rocket launch, have a friend or parent assist by taking the photographs so you can concentrate on what you are doing. Graphs, charts and diagrams, as well as photographic materials, can all be used to visually

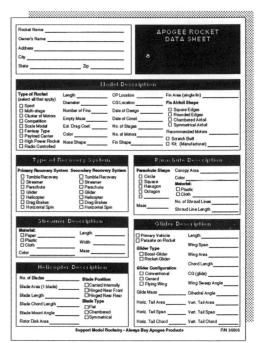

represent your data. Remember, the display is a visual representation of your project. As always, it is better to collect too much data, observations and photos, and have a choice of the best materials, than not to have enough.

The next chapter will help you with data gathering techniques that are specific to model rocket experiments. This usually involves tracking your rocket to record a specific parameter such as height, time aloft, acceleration, or the model's velocity.

## Launch Procedures

Using model rockets in your research project can add some additional conditions that you may need to consider. Many modelers have experience "launch frustration" when launching a rocket. This could be anything from a igniter that fails to ignite the motor, to a parachute that melts into a plastic wad at ejection. This leads to wasted time, and may mean a damaged model.

Preventing "launch frustration" takes planning. Since your science project dictates that things need to be done exactly the same way for each launch, you should already have a set of procedures which you plan to follow. Be sure to include rocket safety steps and pre-liftoff flight checks in your procedures. Not only will this help you keep the launches exactly the same, but it will help eliminate many frustrating or "un-safe" conditions.

Apogee Components has a nice set of procedures called the *"Apogee Countdown Checklist."* You may want to get a copy to assist you in developing your own list of steps. But here are some questions to ask yourself to create your procedures:

1. What are the recommended motors that can be used safely in my rocket?

2. What special tools and/or equipment will be needed to prepare the rocket for flight?

3. What are the special safety precautions that must be considered for the rocket's launch?

4. After the launch is over, what data

should be gathered from the flight itself?

5. As you examine the rocket, what pieces of the model could possibly break that might cause the flight to be a failure? How would you check those parts to make sure that they are safe for flight?

6. Before the rocket is placed on the pad, what items must be performed to prepare the rocket for launch?

7. When you place the rocket on the pad, what items need to be accomplished to make sure the rocket takes off straight when you push the launch button?

8. List any activities that must be performed after the rocket is placed on the launch rod to launch the rocket.

9. What items need to be performed after the launch to make sure the pad area is safe?

10. If the motor fails to ignite, what steps are necessary to make the rocket ready for launch again?

11. Are there any unique steps to perform to recover and return the model in a safe conditions (so that valuable data isn't lost)?

12. How will you record the data collected from the flight?

13. Are there any steps that must be taken after the flight to gather data from the model?

14. What will you have to do between flights to make it ready for the next part of your experiment?

As part of your experiment, you'll want to make a list of similar questions to ask yourself for the preparation of the payload (if any). These procedures will be attached to your final report so that the judges will be able to examine the methods you used to conduct your research.

## The Lab Report

After you have finished gathering all the data from your launches, you are ready to begin the *Lab Report*. The lab report details the scientific method followed in your experiment and all related information on your project. The report consists of the following parts:

1.   The title page.
2.   A statement of the problem.
3.   Your research.
4.   A statement of your hypothesis.
5.   A list of the materials used in your project.

6. The experimental procedure used.
7. The results of your experiment (i.e., the data gathered).
8. A conclusion based upon your results.
9. The bibliography.

Begin compiling your report as you begin, you will find later that the report almost writes itself. Start by writing down your *Problem* and *Hypothesis*. List your materials as you obtain them, include their quantities. List your procedure steps as you develop them. Write data and observations down immediately. It is impossible to accurately remember the results at a later time. Keep a separate list of all sources, including personal contacts, books, magazines, newspapers, television shows and movies. The bibliography should be formatted as in acceptable published guides.

## The Abstract

You may be required to prepare an *abstract* for your science fair project report. The abstract is a short, concise explanation of your science fair project. It should be no longer than one page and can be included in the beginning of your report and placed on the display board. A possible scenario is to use three paragraphs.

Paragraph 1    A brief explanation of the problem you investigated.
Paragraph 2    A brief description of the procedure you followed.
Paragraph 3    A statement about the formulation of your conclusion.

## Display Board and Exhibit

After the Lab Report is completed, you are ready to start the final portion of your project —creating the display for the actual fair. The *display board* should contain the following information:
1. The project title.
2. A statement of the problem.
3. A statement of the hypothesis.
4. A step-by-step procedure, including photographs.
5. The results, including data, observations, graphs, charts and diagrams to visually present your information.
6. Your conclusion(s).
7. The abstract.
The display board is the part of your project that people will see first. The visual

presentation is important and must be attractive. It should be eye catching; displays incorporating motion, sound and additional lighting will help your's "stand apart," like a well constructed advertisement or TV commercial and "invite" visitors to come closer and find out more about your project. Video tape presentations may be a good beginning.

All lettering should be large enough for someone standing at a distance of 3 to 5 feet to read easily. Subject headings should be larger than the text for that section. Adhesive vinyl lettering is neater than hand printing or stenciling and available in various sizes and colors from hobby and art supply stores. Text can be produced, edited and printed using a personal computer. Bordering or mounting text sections and headings on colored backgrounds add to visual appeal.

Graphs, charts and diagrams should be neat, well labeled, produced separately and applied to the display board. Mistakes made directly on the board can become permanent and irreversible, detracting from the presentation. The area in front of the display board is where the lab report and materials are placed. Some components can be supported and placed directly on the board. Be certain you have sufficient support for the display board itself so it doesn't easily tip over.

## Oral Presentation

As a student, you may be required to give an oral presentation of your project. Have all the experimental materials, report and display board ready at the time of your presentation. Use your lab report as a guide, and when you start your presentation identify the title of the project and the experimental problem. Explain the reason for your hypothesis. Describe the procedure you used to conduct the experiment. Present the result you obtained and then state your conclusion. Refer to your research when necessary, as established and documented facts or figures, it will serve as an information source for you to answer questions from the audience.

Practice your presentation before you deliver it to the judges. It will make you more comfortable when it is "your turn" to get up before the audience.

During the presentation, remember to speak clearly and project your voice so that members of the audience seated in the back of the room can hear you. As important, make eye contact with different audience members, as if speaking directly to them. It will improve your presentation and help convey your ideas to an unresponsive audience.

## Evaluation

Your science fair project may be evaluated for an academic grade. Points to consider when selecting a project for content and quality are:

1. Knowledge gained — what knowledge the student gains by conducting the project.
2. Information — is the information collected through research appropriate?
3. Scientific approach — is the *scientific method* applicable, can a controlled variable be used in the project?
4. Collection of data — can measurements be taken accurately?
5. Conclusions — is the conclusion logical and valid?
6. Written report — are the lab report and display board organized and neat?
7. Oral presentation — is the oral report organized and interesting?
8. Exhibit — is the display visually attractive, appealing and captivating?
9. Effort — is the effort considerable and demonstrative?
10. Creativity — how creative is the approach to solving the problem?
11. Originality — has the project been presented recently or performed by other students in the past?

*Portions of this chapter were written by or with the aid of Dr. Bob Kreutz.*

# Chapter 3

# Basic rocketry data gathering techniques

### Data gathering begins with selecting the right topic

Selecting the *right* topic becomes important to the overall success of the project. You should select a topic so that it is easy to see the differences between launches when a variable is changed. As an example, many young students try to relate something like fin shape with how high the rocket will fly. Unfortuneately this type of project will be very difficult to get data from which you can make an accurate conclusion—because the results from each flight will be very similar. If the person had an some knowledge in aeronautics, they would know that fin shape has little to do with the altitude achieved by a rocket. What is more important is the shape of the fin's *cross section*; a streamlined fin will travel a lot higher than one with just square edges. But nearly every modeler knows this second fact, while most don't know the first, and assume it would be a great topic to exlore.

This is where doing research is important. Not only should you do research to find a topic that can be explored "conclusively" with model rockets, but you should also find out what has been explored previously. If you don't know what was done in past, you may end up repeating the same failed experiments. Through this research you may also find a different way to approach the topic being explored which you might not have thought about before.

Nearly every science fair project listed in this book gives some areas that can be explored indepth with additional researched. You can use the section at the end of this book if you don't know *where* to find the information to start your background search. It lists several excellent places where technical information can be found for various topics involving model rocketry.

### Gathering Data when flying your rocket

When you launch your rocket, it is going to do something — it will take off and fly successfully, or it will fail to perform correctly in one way or another. But whatever happens, there is a lot of information available from which you can make some conclusions. But to use this data, you must record it. It is too easy to forget what happened on *Flight #2* after you have just finished *Flight #12*.

The best way to record what happens when the rocket takes off is to write it down on some type of *data* sheet. You can easily make your own data sheet and record all the parameters of the flight that you think are important and which describe the way the rocket performed or you can also use a data sheet produced by one of the model rocket companies. If you choose the later, I suggest the *"Apogee Flight Record"* from Apogee Components. This 'check-box' form contains over

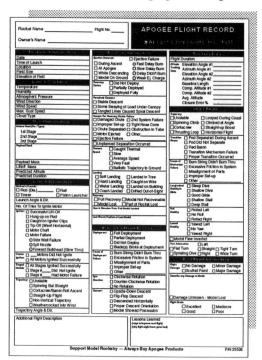

170 possible flight events that may occur when the rocket takes off. To use it, you simply observe the flight and make a mark in the appropriate box that describes what happened. When done, you will have a complete record of what happened on that particular flight. You can even take this data and write a narrative description for that flight.

Apogee Components also has a companion publication: *"Technical Publication #9, Analyzing a Model Rocket's Flight"* which can be used to assist you in determining why a rocket performed the way it did. This is extremely helpful if the flight was not as you anticipated. If the models are consistently flying in the same manner, you may want to change the design of the rocket, or modify the procedures you are using to launch the model. But analyzing the flight is the starting point to see if changes are needed.

You may also want to collect additional data on the rocket's flight and measure some other specific parameters. The two most common recorded parameters are: the model's peak altitude, and how long it stayed in the air. This act of recording how your rocket performed is called "tracking" the model.

## Tracking Your Rocket

If your science project involves launching two or more rockets of different sizes or shapes, you will probably need to know how high the rockets fly. Knowing how high the rocket flew will allow you to make a comparison of which shape is better, or why your data may have yielded different results for models you thought should have been the same.

*Tracking* a rocket for science fair projects is challenging. There are many variables affecting the rocket as it takes off, each of which could skew the data. Here are just some of the things that could affect the rocket's flight and therefore your data:

A. A gust of wind could come up and tilt the trajectory of the rocket, making it's apogee (highest point) less than what it could have been.
B. Rocket motors of the same type can differ by a small amount. Because of this small difference, the same rocket will reach a slightly different altitude when launched repeatedly.
C. Air pressure and temperature affect the density of the air, which changes the drag on a model. So if you can't launch two rockets at the same time, you will really have a hard time making an accurate comparison.

Because of these and other variables, it would be better for you to launch the rockets *many* times and calculate an *average* altitude for the models. By taking an average, you will reduce the effect of all those little variables (such as gusts of wind) which you can't control. This "average" altitude would be used to make your final conclusions.

## Altitude Determination: Method #1 - The Drop Mass

The easiest — but least accurate — method of determining the altitude of your rocket is to drop an object from it that falls at a constant rate. When the object falls at a constant rate, such as 1.5 meters per second, you can simply time the object from when it ejects from the model until it touches down on the ground. Then you multiply this time by the rate at which it falls. For example, if it takes 100 seconds for the object to fall, and it has a constant descent rate of 1.5 meter per second, then the approximate altitude of the rocket when it ejected the object would be 150 meters (1.5 m/s X 100 s).

What kinds of objects can you use in this simple altitude determination method? A small streamer attached to washer as shown in the drawing works well. The streamer is then simply rolled up and inserted into the body of the rocket. When the rocket deploys the parachute, it also kicks out the streamer.

Finding out the rate at which the streamer falls is also fairly simple. Just drop it from high platform (of a known height) and record how long it takes it to hit the

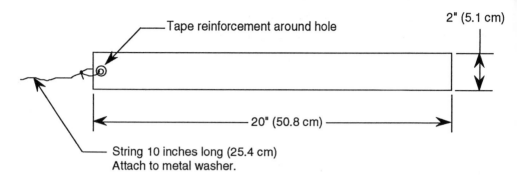

Tape reinforcement around hole

2" (5.1 cm)

20" (50.8 cm)

String 10 inches long (25.4 cm)
Attach to metal washer.

ground. Indoor locations are best, because you don't have to worry about air updrafts skewing the measurements. For example, you might drop it from a high balcony or from the rafters in a gymnasium. The descent rate is then the height divided by the time it took to fall to the ground.

If you use this method, you will also have to make a couple of notes in your final report. You'll want to include those things that can make this altitude measurement system inaccurate. These can include the rocket not being at peak altitude when the streamer deploys; the streamer being caught in a thermal and therefore not falling at a constant rate; and the streamer falls fast until it unfurls, and then takes some time to slow down to its constant descent rate.

A way to improve the accuracy of the streamer method is to perform multiple launches with the same model so a large number of flights might be averaged. The greater the number of flights made, the more consistent the results.

### Altitude Determination: Method #2 - Optical tracking

Because it is more accurate, optical tracking is a better method of finding out how high a rocket flies. In this method, you sight the model at the highest point, and not when the ejection charge occurs. Most often, the ejection charge does not occur exactly at the apogee of the flight. This is the major flaw in the simpler "drop streamer" method, because it assumes the model is at its highest point when the streamer is released.

Optical tracking requires that you to make a simple tracking scope and take angular measurements. From this, you perform some trigonometric calculations to determine how high the rocket was when the measurement was taken.

The advantages of optical tracking are: it is more accurate than drop mass method, and that it is very inexpensive to perform (simple tracking scopes can be made out of readily available materials). The disadvantage is that this methods requires a lot of practice in order to get good results.

The simple paper tracking scope from Apogee Components (P/N 35511) is really easy to use, and does not require any math to determine how high the rocket flew. As the illustration shows, you simply stand back from the launch pad by 100 meters, and then record the angle on the tracking scope for maximum height of the model. You then take this angle and using the supplied "Altitude Calculator" card, simply read off the height of the model. See the figure on next page.

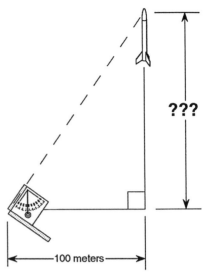

**Optical tracking of a rocket**

The most accurate system involves at least two tracking stations taking both elevation and azimuth angles. I suggest reading the following two reports from the National Association of Rocketry that discuss this method in greater detail:

**#1) Optical Tracking System**
Publication Number: TR-3    $0.85

**A simple tracking scope**

**#2) Tracking** - A collection of articles including altitude tracking and data reduction, two station tracking and Triple-Track Tracker. Publication Number: TR-107    $2.00

These reports are available from:

National Association of Rocketry Technical Service
P.O. Box 1482

Saugus, MA 01906

## *Wind Tunnel Experiments*

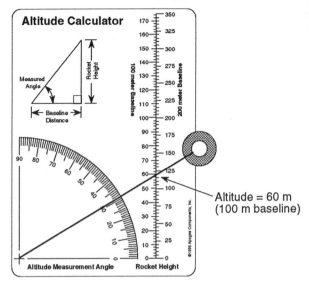

When your experiment requires that you compare one rocket shape to another, a better method than measuring altitude is to use a wind tunnel. This method places the rocket into a controlled airstream, and you can directly measure the drag and other forces acting on the model. By knowing the drag of the model, you can conclude that the shape with the lowest drag (or lowest coefficient of drag) will fly the highest.

Determining actual forces on the model; such as lift and drag, are the *best* use of wind tunnels in rocketry experiments. From these measurements you can calculated the coefficient of lift ($C_l$) and coefficient of drag ($C_d$) for the model being tested. These two parameters are used to compare one model against the other — such as your control model against the one you think is an improved version.

The problem or disadvantage associated with the use of a wind tunnel method is that *good* wind tunnels are very expensive to build. If the airflow in the tunnel isn't smooth, uniform, and at a velocity that a typical rocket flies at, the data will be inconsistent at best, and most likely it will be useless for making comparisons. Additionally, the actual forces on a model rocket are very small, and are difficult to measure without accurate test equipment. This also adds to the expense of the wind tunnel.

If this method looks like the best way to perform your experiment, it is advisable that you contact a large college or university which has a wind tunnel. If you can obtain permission to use their wind tunnel, you

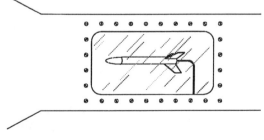

**Model rocket in a wind tunnel**

will also be able to get assistance from one of the college professors on how to use the wind tunnel, and how to collect and interpret the data. They will also tell you the specific information about how models should be built so that they will fit and also work properly in their wind tunnel.

Those interested in finding explanations of the various types of wind tunnels and measurement systems, as well as information on designing and building wind tunnels should read the book titled *Wind Tunnel Testing*, by Alan Pope, published by John Wiley & Sons.

### Coefficient of Drag Estimation from Altitude Measurements

Besides using a wind tunnel, another way to determine the $C_d$ of a model is to use the process of "reverse engineering." In this method, you start by launching the model and determine how high it flew using optical tracking techniques. From the maximum altitude of the rocket, you then run simulations with computer software to estimate the coefficient of drag to reach this altitude.

In using this computer software, you must input the motor used, the diameter of the model, and the $C_d$ of the model to determine the altitude. Since you don't

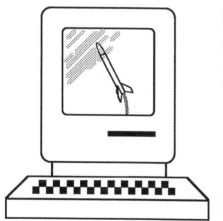

know the $C_d$, you make a guess (start with 0.75) and see what the altitude would be as predicted by the program. You then modify the $C_d$ to make the predicted altitude on the computer closer to the actual tracked altitude. You keep making guesses until the the predicted altitude is equal to the actual measurement. Eventually, you will end up with a fairly accurate $C_d$ for the model.

As you can easily conclude, this method relies on the computer being able to accurately predict the altitude of the rocket with the given parameters. There are many variables that can make the predicted altitude from the computer wrong; such as: the actual motors used may not produce the anticipated amount of thrust, or the model not flying a near-vertical trajectory. Fortunately, most of the computer programs are accurate enough to make generalized comparisions.

The computer programs to predict the altitude of a model rocket are common and easy to find. There are several programs available on the Internet and other computer networks. Or you can contact Apogee Components for further information if you don't know where to start looking for one.

## Timing Data

Measuring how long a rocket stays in the air, or how long it takes it to fall is an easy way to get usable data on which to base your conclusions. The only equipment you'll need is a keen eye and a stopwatch. Many wrist watches have built in stop-watch functions, so you may already have all the equipment you need.

As discussed in the *Altitude Determination: Method #1 - The Drop Mass* section, you may even be able to use the timing technique to get an approximation of how high the rocket flew. For example, if you had an object that is dropped out of a rocket and falls at a predetermined rate, say 9 meters per second, and it takes 20 seconds for it to fall, you would know that the rocket was at an altitude of 180 meters (180 = 9 X 20) when the object was released.

Timing data is best used when comparing the descent rates of two different recovery systems. If you have two streamers, and they were both dropped from the same model (and at the same time), you could easily conclude that the streamer that hit the ground *last* had the slowest descent rate. This technique would be best used in experiments where you were trying to improve on the recovery system used by the rocket.

The problem with timing data is that it can also be inconsistent. For example, if the launch occurs on a windy day, it could change how fast the object falls. Additionally, rising columns of warm air, called *thermals*, will slow the descent rate of the object. To get better results, you will have to make multiple flights to find an average. This "average" descent time would then be used to make comparisions.

A better method when making comparisions between two different recovery systems is to drop them from the same model at the same time. Since both "test articles" will fall from the exact same height, and through the same air (thermals, wind, etc.), then you can make direct comparisions with a higher degree of accuracy and confidence. This will also cut down on the number of launches needed to complete the experiment.

## Measuring Velocity and Acceleration

There are many experiments that could be performed which would require that you know the acceleration or velocity of the rocket as it takes off. For example, if you were studying the effects of acceleration on a tadpole or if you were trying to find out if a rocket using a piston launcher had a higher launch velocity than a rocket without one; you would need a method to determine these parameters.

Velocity and acceleration are very closely related, because accleration is a "change in velocity" of the object being studied. So measuring velocity and/or acceleration are done in the same way. There are two methods that are commonly used in rocketry: an onboard sensing and measuring system, or some type of optical tracking.

The onboard sensing and measuring system is some type of mechanical or electrical device that measures directly the acceleration of the rocket. This payload device is called an *accelerometer*. There are two types of accelerometers, mechanical, and electronic.

Mechanical accelerometers consist of a large heavy *mass* (such as a lead block) mounted on a spring. When the model lifts off, the "weight" of the material increases because of the acceleration of the rocket—which compresses the spring. The amount that the spring compresses is proportional to the increase in acceleration of the rocket. So a simple accelerometer can be constructed from a small spring and a heavy mass. The drawback to this type of accelerometer is that it only records the "greatest" acceleration experienced during the flight. So the usefullness is limited to only certain experiments.

Electronic accelerometers are much more versatile, and some of the better ones can be used to record the acceleration of the model throughout the entire flight. Another advantage of electronic accelerometers is that they can be very accurate. The drawback to electronic accelerometers is that they are very expensive. They are also fairly heavy — they need a battery and other electronic components to record the information. Because of this they need larger rockets and also, bigger, more expensive motors, to lift them into the air.

There are basically two types of electronic accelerometers; those measuring just the peak acceleration of the rocket, and those that continually measure and store the acceleration throughout the entire flight. This second type of accelerometer is very useful because it contains so much information, and from this data, you can even calculate the altitude of the model, and also the drag force acting on the rocket.

Accelerometers can be obtained from manufacturers that specialize in electronic payloads for rockets. I suggest that you obtain a *"High Power Rocketry"* magazine, and look through the advertisements for those firms that make these products. Expect to pay at least $80 for a simple electronic accelerometer.

### Measuring acceleration using optical tracking

A less accurate way, but much less expensive way to measure velocity and acceleration is through *optical tracking*. Optical tracking was explained in a previous section as a way to determine the height of a model. If you haven't already done so, you should read through that section to familiarize yourself with the basic priciples and methods involved — as they will be needed and used to find the acceleration or velocity of the model.

Below are several methods of optical tracking that may yield usable results for your experiment.

### Method 1: Average velocity from liftoff to peak altitude.

In this method, you not only take the angular measurements to determine the peak altitude of the model, but at the same time, you record how long if took for the model to reach this altitude. The average velocity during the flight is then the peak altitude height divided by the time you measured for the model to reach this altitude.

$$\text{Avg. Velocity} = \frac{\text{Height}}{\text{Time}}$$

It is also possible to find the average descent velocity of the model by recording the time it took the model to descend to the ground from its peak height. You then divide the peak altitude measurement by the time it took to descend to the ground; which will give the average descent velocity of the model, which might be useful for comparing different recovery devices.

### Method 2: Average velocity or acceleration of a model to reach a certain height.

This method differs from the first method in that you don't measure the peak altitude to which the rocket flew, but how long it took to reach a certain level in the sky. The velocity of the rocket is found by dividing this altitude by the time it took to reach this altitude.

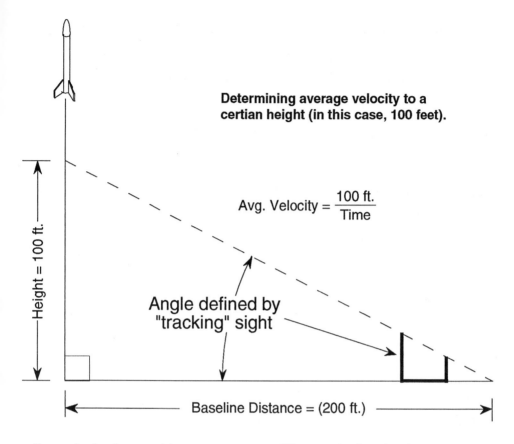

**Determining average velocity to a certian height (in this case, 100 feet).**

$$\text{Avg. Velocity} = \frac{100 \text{ ft.}}{\text{Time}}$$

Height = 100 ft.

Angle defined by "tracking" sight

Baseline Distance = (200 ft.)

Instead of using tracking scopes, you will use a device that lets you mark a specific point in the sky. Such a device, like the one shown in the illustration on the next page can be constructed from PVC pipes, or scraps of wood staked into the ground.

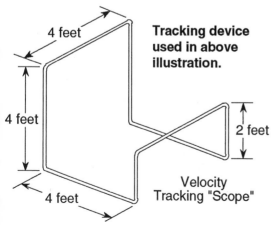

**Tracking device used in above illustration.**

4 feet

4 feet

2 feet

4 feet

Velocity Tracking "Scope"

The purpose of the special device (shown to the left) is to define a set altitude in the sky. The bars define an angle, so it is very similar to using a altitude tracking scope. By knowing the distance from the pad to the device, you they multiply this length by the tangent of the angle of the device, you will know the height of the "point" in the sky. The device shown in these illustrations works by defining an altitude of 100 feet in the air, so you don't really need to know any trigonometry at all to determine the average velocity of the rocket. You simply divide 100 feet by the amount of time it took to reach the altitude.

To use this device, the person tracking the rocket lays down on the ground under the uneven bars with their head near the lowest bar. The person should look upward across the bars so the lower (front) bar blocks the view of the higher bar. This will define an exact altitude in the sky when the distance is known from the launch pad to the person doing the tracking (in the illustration, it is 200 feet).

When the rocket is launched, the tracker simply times it from the instant it leaves the pad to when it crosses the line of sight which is defined by the parallel bars. The average velocity of the rocket as it crosses this point in the sky is equal to the altitude "point" divided by the time it took to reach the point in the sky.

For example, if it took 1.3 seconds to travel 100 feet, the average velocity for the model would be $100 \div 1.3 = 76.9$ feet/sec (23.4 m/sec).

With two different trackers (each timing to two different altitudes), you can also get an average acceleration between the two points in the sky.

Average acceleration would be equal to the change in velocity between the two points divided by the differences in time between the two trackers. So if the first tracker found it took 1.3 seconds to travel 100 feet, and the second tracker found it took 2.8 seconds to travel *200 feet*, then the following results could be calculated:

Average velocity for tracker #1 = 76.9 feet/sec;

Average velocity for tracker #2 = 71.4 feet/sec.

Then the acceleration between the points would be:

$$a = (v_2 - v_1) / (t_2 - t_1)$$

$$a = (71.4 - 76.9) / (2.8 - 1.3) = -3.66 \text{ feet} / s^2$$

The fact that this is a negative number means the rocket is decelerating, or slowing down. This means that the rocket was already in its coast phase. *(Typically, while the motor is thrusting, the acceleration will always be a positive number.)*

Important note: this is not the actual acceleration of the model, but only an indication of what the rocket is experiencing. The reason is that the velocities were not actual velocities, but *average* velocities between the two points in the sky.

*Method 3: Tracking with a video camera*

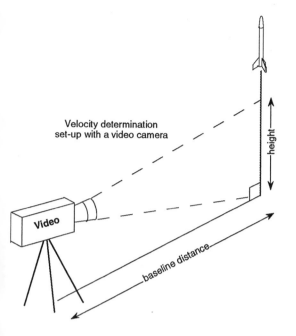

Velocity determination
set-up with a video camera

baseline distance

height

Video

This method is similar to the second method, except a video camera is used to record the flight, which is then analyzed at a later time to determine average velocity.

The video camera is set up on a tripod so the rocket is low in the view field of the camera before it is launched. The camera should be stationary, and not be touched or moved during the flight. When the rocket lifts off, it will fly through the view of the camera and should fly off the screen of the viewfinder. Do not move the camera between launches - only turn it on and off to save tape.

The velocity is found in a similar way as method 2. You review the flight, and measure the time from lift-off to when the model exits the screen. Since the top of the "frame" is marking a certain altitude in the sky, the average velocity is this altitude divided by the time it was visible in the on-screen once it lifted off.

### Calibrating the Video Equipment

If you use this method, you must first determine the *view angle* of the lens by taking a calibration shot. This lens angle, labeled "α" (alpha) in the illustration on the next page, is necessary to know in order to find the height of the rocket during the actual launch of your model. The calibration shot should be of an object of known height — such as a flagpole. You may have to determine the height of the flagpole by using other methods (such as the triangulation technique used to find a rocket's altitude). Once the height is known, here are the steps involved in calibrating the equipment for the experiment. The entire purpose of this calibration procedure is to find angle α (alpha).

1. Mount the camera on a tripod. If the camera has a zoom feature, then zoom out (fully) so that objects appear small in the viewfinder.
2. Center the "test" object (a flagpole of known height) in the field of view of the camera.

**Determining velocity with a video camera**

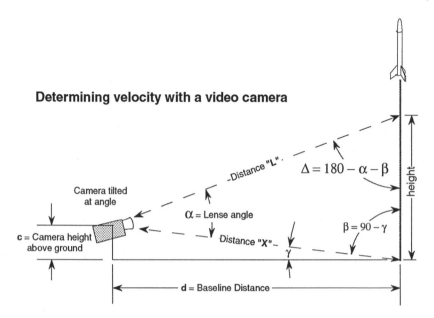

3. Move the camera forward or backward so that the height of the object just fills the entire vertical view of the camera. Tilt the camera vertically if necessary, and lock the camera in this "tilted" position.
4. Measure the height of the camera above the ground (distance "**c**" in the illustration).
5. Measure the baseline (distance "**d**" in the illustration) from the base of the "test" object to the center of the tripod along the ground. Use a long tape measure to get an accurate measurement.
6. Calculate distance "**x**" from the following formula:

$$x = \sqrt{c^2 + d^2}$$

7. Calculate angle $\gamma$ (gamma) from the following equation:

$$\gamma = \tan^{-1}\left(\frac{c}{d}\right)$$

8. Calculate angle B (Beta) from the following equation:

$$B = 90° - \gamma$$

9. Find distance "L" from the following equation.

$$L = \sqrt{h^2 + x^2 - 2\,h\,x\,\cos B}$$

10. Find angle $\alpha$ (alpha) from the following equation:

# Basic rocketry data gathering techniques

$$\alpha = \sin^{-1}\left(\frac{h \sin B}{L}\right)$$

Once the lens angle $\alpha$ (alpha) is found, you can now track your rockets with the video camera to determine average velocity of your models. Before you begin, you will have to perform some set-up steps.

## Setting up the camera to take velocity measurements

The purpose of setting up the camera with these steps is so that you can accurately determine the elevation in the sky where the rocket will exit the view of the camera.

1. Set up the launch pad. Stake it into the ground so that it is not moved between launches.
2. Mount the camera on a tripod. If the camera has a zoom feature, then zoom out (fully) so that objects appear small in the viewfinder.
3. Position the camera far back from the launch pad. You may have to experiment with the actual distance, but it might be good to start at 50 meters. You want the rocket to be in the field of view of the camera for at least one full second when it lifts off so it is easier to make time measurements when reviewing the tape later.
4. Measure the distance from the launch pad to the center of the tripod along the ground. Use a long tape measure to get an accurate distance measurement.
5. Tilt the camera vertically on the tripod so that the launch pad is at the bottom of the "field of view" of the camera. Lock the camera in this "tilted" position, and do not move the camera until "*all*" the test flights are over. Only turn the camera off and on between launches to save batteries and tape.
6. Measure the height of the camera above the ground (distance "c" in the illustration).
7. Calculate distance "x" from the following formula:

$$x = \sqrt{c^2 + d^2}$$

8. Calculate angle $\gamma$ (gamma) from the following equation:

$$\gamma = \tan^{-1}\left(\frac{c}{d}\right)$$

9. Calculate angle B (Beta) from the following equation:

$$B = 90° - \gamma$$

10. Calculate angle $\Delta$ (Delta) from the following equation:

$$\Delta = 180° - \alpha - B$$

11. Calculate the "height" of the rocket as it crosses out of the view of the camera with the following formula:

$$h = \left(\frac{x}{\sin \Delta}\right) \sin \alpha$$

Once this height is known, you are now ready to start flying your rockets. Launches should be straight up, and not angled in any way. If the flights were not completely vertical, this would make the average velocity lower. You can launch your rockets using this method without worrying about recording any data during the launch sequence. Once you know the "height," you can determine the average velocity later - so that launches can proceed at a faster pace.

When reviewing the tape, you will start timing from the moment you see the rocket move to when it exits the top of the field of view of the camera. Many times you might only see a blur and a smoke trail. Moving the camera further away from the launch pad will help make the rocket easier to time. The average velocity is the "height" divided by the time it took to exit the camera's field of view.

The advantage of having the flight recorded on video tape is that you can review it several times, and repeat your velocity calculations, so results can be more accurate.

Like method #2, you can use two cameras to track the same rocket between two different altitudes, and then you can also get an average accleration of the model.

With some expensive cameras, and with frame-by-frame viewing, you may also be able to determine acceleration of the rocket between frames too. This would make an excellent science fair project for those individuals who have this type of equipment.

## Measuring lift-off velocity using a video camera

It is also possible to use a video camera to make measurements of the velocity of the rocket at lift-off. This might be useful for projects comparing one type of launch system to another (i.e., a tower launcher vs. a piston launcher - see Experiment #25). Another project might be comparing two different motors.

The video camera is used very close to the pad, and the calibration steps explained previously are not required. Instead, you will mount a long ruler next to the rocket so you can measure how far the rocket moved during a given time.

Because the rocket moves very fast, you will need a VCR with frame-by-frame viewing. If you know the time between each frame (consult the owner's manual of the VCR), and the distanced the rocket moved, then the velocity of the rocket is: Distance ÷ Time.

# Chapter 4

# Project Ideas: 43 *Experiments*

This section is a list of many good topics that can be studied with the aid of model rocketry; which is probably the reason you are reading this book. You want to use rockets because you have a great interest in them, but you need to know exactly what things you can do with them that make a good and interesting science fair project. Be of good cheer; there are more topics that can be studied than can be listed in this book. This list is primarily of aeronautics topics that can be explored through the use of model rockets. By the time you go through this section, you will probably think of several more good experiments that could be added. That is the real purpose of this list — to develop a topic of your own creation.

The list of 69 science fair topics is broken down into two categories: experiments and demonstrations. *Experiments* are projects where you may not be able to accurately predict the outcome. An example might be a project to develop a streamer that falls slower than a "standard" one. Your goal is to gather good data that can be analyzed to see if a pattern develops, so that you can make some kind of definite conclusion.

*Demonstration projects* are typically easier than the experimental projects. In these projects, you know the outcome because you have researched the topic and have a knowledge of the principles involved. Such a project might be: *"I predict that a low mass rocket will fly higher than a heavier one."* The list of *Demonstration Projects* will be described in the next chapter.

Many science fair projects will allow demonstration projects because they are excellent at teaching the *scientific method* (see chapter 2) to younger students. But check with your teacher to make sure that these types of projects are allowed before you start them.

## *Hints and Tips on Good Projects*

Before you jump to the list, here are some hints and tips that will make your rocketry related science fair project easier and more enjoyable.

1. You will probably be working under a financial budget, and you may be tempted to use a small rocket. Don't! Use the largest rocket that you can still afford.

Larger rockets are easier to see when flying (hence; easier to track), and are less likely to be lost.

2. Select a rocket motor which allows the rocket to fly slow enough to be *easily* tracked. These are typically low "average thrust" rocket motors (not merely smaller rocket motors). Apogee Components' High Performance Model Rocket Motors have a low thrust level, and are great for slow — easy-to-track flights.

3. Build the model with extra durability. Since you will be launching it many many times, it must be able to survive a lot of hard landings. If the model needs to be repaired between flights, you will be changing it, and thus the results of the data may be skewed in favor of those flights that were flown with a undamaged model.

4. As stated before, keep the project simple. The fewer the variables, the more accurate the results will be, and the faster the experimentation phase of the project. This will help you keep your focus, and it will make the entire project go much quicker too.

5. Don't procrastinate — start the project quickly. While performing your research you may be contacting several people to get information. If they will be sending you something in the mail, it may take a while for the package to get to you. This may take the longest time of the entire project, so the sooner you get this step over, the easier it will be to perform the rest of your project. Besides, *rocket people* are very fun to talk with and are very helpful, so don't be afraid or hesitate to contact them.

6. Make as many flights as possible. This may be tough when you are on a limited budget, but the results and conclusions will be easier to reach and verify at the end of the project.

7. Whenever possible, try to make *generalized* "design rules." This will help you with future rocket projects to make projections on different models. For example, if you were exploring fins size, you would not want to conclude your report by saying: *"Make fins 12 cm long, and 12 cm wide."* This would only allow you to make a certain size model. A better approach would be to relate the fin dimensions to the size of the rocket. For example, you might find that: *"fins should be made 1.5 D long, and 1.5 D wide; where "D" is the diameter of the model."*

## Types of Research Experiments

There are many different types of experiments that can be performed with model rocketry. Since model rocketry mimics the real world of aeronautics and space exploration, you can perform similar experiments that are done with full size (professional) rockets. So try to find out what NASA and other scientific organizations launch as experiments. This will always be a good starting point in selecting a topic for your science fair project.

Typically, NASA and other organizations classify payloads in any of several areas called *sciences*. You may have heard talk about *life sciences, material sciences*, or *environmental sciences*. These areas of concentration can be duplicated to one degree or another in model rocketry.

The following list of topics for science fair projects are chiefly involved with *aeronautics* and *rocket propulsion*. Most of the topics are self-explanatory, while other are slightly more complex to describe. Where necessary, a short background will be given on the topic, as well as some hints on where to start the project, what research you may need, and how to conduct the project so you get meaningful results.

Reviewing this list of topics, you may be interested more in one area than another. As you study the particular area that interests you, you will probably see other topics that can be further researched. Try to come up with a new topic, because then you can take pride in calling the idea your own.

## Streamer Recovery Systems #1

**Project**: Develop an improved streamer that descends slower.

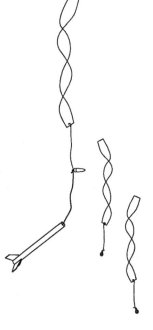

### Background:

Streamers are typically used on smaller rockets because they fall fairly fast and don't drift very far on breezy days. But because they fall faster than a parachute, heavier models can be damaged from hard landings. This project would be to design and test a new type of streamer that would fall slower than a "control" streamer. An improved streamer would allow for this type of recovery to be used safely on larger or heavier models, and still prevent the model from drifting too far in a breeze.

Your "control" streamer should be as simple as possible; a strip of plastic rolled up would be better than one folded in some way. The "improved" streamer should be made from the same material and have the same amount of area as the control version (to limit the number of variables), but somehow made better.

This experiment can proceed faster if you attach a metal washer to your streamers and drop two from the same rocket at the same time. This would allow you to tell which streamer fell slower, and then you don't have to track or time the models; since you can easily determine which performed better.

The rocket should have its own recovery device as shown in the illustration.

## Where to Start:

The book *Model Rocket Design & Construction* describes a simple design criteria from which you can make your control streamer. It suggest using a streamer with an area of 8.5 square centimeters per gram of returned rocket mass. The length-to-width ratio of a typical streamer is approximately 10-to-1.

For ideas on how to modify a streamer to make it fall slower, I suggest that you start with Apogee Components' *Technical Publication #4 — The Science & Beauty of Streamer Recovery*. It has a variety of folding techniques and other suggestions that can be a good start for ideas on how to make your "improved" streamer. This publication will also help you generate your own topics for other new streamer experiments.

**Rocket Experiment 2**

## Streamer Recovery Systems #2

**Project**: Will two streamers make a rocket fall slower than just one?

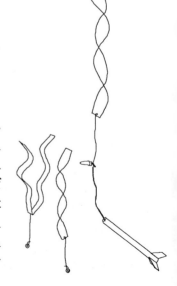

## Background:

Streamers are typically used on smaller rockets because they fall fairly fast and don't drift as far in breezy conditions. Because they fall faster than a parachute, the model can be damaged as a result of hard landings. This project would be to perform a test to see whether two streamers attached to a model will fall slower than a single streamer with equal area. An improved streamer would allow this type of recovery to be used safely on larger models, and still prevent the model from drifting too far in a breeze.

You will want to determine if the interaction between two streamers creates more drag than a single streamer. If there is an improvement, you may want to also try to determine if increases in length of the steamer (use length-to-width ratio) will help or reduce any benefit achieved.

Instead of timing the rockets individually, it is possible to attach a metal washer to your different streamers, so that they can be dropped from the rocket at the same time. This would allow you to tell which streamer fell slower, and eliminating any variables that could skew the data from multiple launches.

## Where to Start:

The book *Model Rocket Design & Construction* describes a simple design criteria from which you can make your control streamer. It suggest using a streamer with an area of 8.5 square centimeters per gram of return rocket mass. The length-to-width ratio of a typical streamer is approximately 10-to-1.

**Rocket Experiment 3**

## Streamer Recovery Systems #3

**Project**: Determine the best area for a streamer.

## Background:

Streamers are typically used on smaller rockets because they fall fairly fast and don't drift too far in breezy conditions. But what should be the *minimum* size of the streamer for a given mass of the descending rocket? Is there also a maximum size (where there is no advantage by making it too larger)?

In performing this experiment, you should first determine the typical rate at which a streamer falls, and then determine how this rate changes with an increase or decrease in the area of the streamer.

You might also see if changes to the length-to-width ratio of the streamer affects the descent rate (with areas being equal). Instead of timing the rockets individually, it is possible to attach a metal washer to your different streamers, so that they can be dropped from the rocket at the same time. This would allow you to tell which streamer falls slower (be sure to make the streamers different colors

so that it is easier to tell them apart when they fall).

## Where to Start:

The book *Model Rocket Design & Construction* describes a simple design criteria from which you can make your control streamer. It suggest using a streamer with an area of 8.5 square centimeters per gram of return rocket mass. The length-to-width ratio of a typical streamer is approximately 10-to-1. It is up to you to decide if this is the best size and area for an "improved" streamer.

**Rocket Experiment 4**

## Parachute Recovery Systems #1

**Project**: Determine if a cluster of parachutes is better than a single parachute.

## Background:

Parachutes are used whenever slow descent speeds are required to soften the landing of a model rocket. By performing this project you would try to determine if two or three small parachutes used together would lower the descent rate of the model compared to a single parachute (with the same surface area).

The possible advantages of this would be slower speeds, and increased safety — because a single parachute that fails to open would cause a serious safety situation; while if two where used and one fails to open, the remaining chute would still bring the model down safely (although slightly faster). Another advantage would be that larger parachutes are more difficult to make, and are therefore more expensive than a few smaller ones.

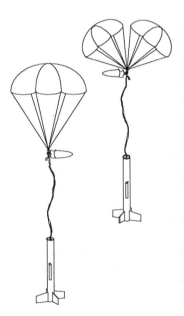

## Where to Start:

The book *Model Rocket Design & Construction* describes how to determine the size of a parachute for a desired descent speed. You'll also want to look in your library for books on parachutes.

**Rocket Experiment 5**

## Parachute Recovery Systems #2

**Project**: Develop a slower descending parachute.

## Background:

Parachutes are used whenever slow descent speeds are required to soften the landing of a model rocket. For many applications, the descent speed is not slow enough — such as for very delicate payloads. Typically, there is only a set volume inside a rocket that can be used to hold a parachute, so using a larger parachute is not always possible. This project would be to develop a parachute with the same size as the control parachute, but that falls at a slower rate.

To start your project, you will have to determine the descent rate of a typical "control" parachute by a series of drops tests. These drop tests can be done from a high balcony, where the chute is timed from release to when it hits the floor. New designs can also be tested this way. The object is to develop a parachute with a slower descent rate than the control parachute.

Be sure that you do fly your "improved" parachute in a rocket. You may find that is migh have some bad deployment characteristics that may make it un-usable in most models.

## Where to Start:

The book *Model Rocket Design & Construction* describes how to determine the size of a parachute for a desired descent speed. You'll also want to look in your library for other books on parachutes.

Apogee Components' *Technical Publication #3 — Increasing the Descent Time of Rocket Parachutes* will give you some ideas of where to start in creating your improved parachute such as trying new materials and using different shapes. It will also give you many other ideas for science fair topics involving parachutes.

## Parachute Recovery Systems #3

**Project**: Develop a steerable parachute.

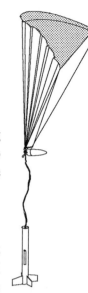

### Background:

Because parachutes fall fairly slow, they tend to drift long distances, making recovery difficult. This project would be to develop a parachute that could be remotely controlled so that the parachute could be steered to a predetermined landing area.

### Where to Start:

Check your libraries for books on parachutes and books about RC airplane control systems. You'll will want to use radio control equipment because it allows direct control of the model while it is still in the air.

## Parachute Recovery Systems #4

**Project**: Determine the strength of the typical plastic parachute.

### Background:

In model rocketry, parachutes are commonly made from polyethylene plastic. The problem with them is that they rip or shred when they open at high speeds. In performing this experiment, you will determine the maximum speed at which a model can be traveling so that the parachute can safely open without being damaged. You should also determine the minimum speed required for the chute to open and inflate fully.

This test might be performed while driving down the highway in an automobile and letting the chute open outside the window (while holding onto the strings of

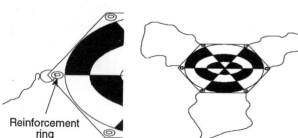

Reinforcement ring

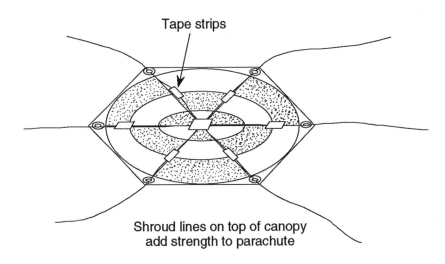

Tape strips

Shroud lines on top of canopy
add strength to parachute

the chute). These tests might be video taped for further analysis. Your set-up should be the same for each test, as you don't want your hand blocking the wind from hitting the parachute when it starts to open.

A better set-up method would be to use an actual rocket body tube. Pack the parachute into the tube, and blow it out (like it would be done in an actual launch). This would more closely simulate what actually happens during a real launch.

After you have determined the maximum safe opening speed of the parachute, you might experiment with ways of attaching the shroud lines (tape or rings), and methods of increasing the strength (looping the lines over the top as shown in the illustration).

A further version of this experiment is to find out what happens if the parachute is made larger? Will it damage more easily? Does the maximum safe opening speed change?

## Where to Start:

The book *Model Rocket Design & Construction* describes a how to determine the size of a parachute for a desired descent speed. It also describes how to build a basic parachute out of commonly available materials (trash bags and plastic drop cloths). You'll also want to look in your library for other books on parachutes.

Rocket
Experiment

# 8

## Parachute Recovery Systems #5

**Project**: Develop a parachute system that allows a change in the descent rate of the model, so it stays in the air for only a predetermined amount of time.

## Background:

Many rocketeers compete in contests where it is desirable for the model to stay in the air for a predetermined time. Or, sometimes a model will get caught in a thermal (a rising column of warm air) and may start to drift away. In both of these cases a system that changes a parachute's descent rate, from slow to fast, is needed. The intent of this project is to develop a "dethermalizer" system that would make this change at a predetermined time, so the model would fall slow initially, and then fall faster to keep the model from drifting too far.

The system would two parts: the timer, and the method that changes the parachutes shape so that it descends faster. This could be as simple as releasing several of the suspension (shroud) lines so the air spills out one side of the parachute. The *timer system* is needed to control when, during the flight, the descent rate is changed. This would make the parachute fall slow initially, then fall faster later.

Another variation of this project is to use a similar system on high altitude models. To keep them from drifting too far, you may want them to initially fall quickly down to some predetermined level. Then they would be slowed down to make a safe and soft landing.

## Where to Start:

The book *Model Rocket Design and Construction* has some suggestions on how to use a dethermalizer on gliders. It may be possible to modify one of these systems to use on a parachute.

Also contact other modelers through the National Association of Rocketry or on the INTERNET for other hints and suggestions on how you might make a determalizer for parachutes.

## Parachute Recovery Systems #6

**Project**: Determine the best folding techniques for parachutes.

### Background:

Folding a parachute is a critical part to the success of a rocket's flight. If it is folded incorrectly, it may not open, and the model could fall too fast. Additionally, in many rocket competitions, a parachute should open quickly so that the model stays in the air for as long as possible. If it takes too long for the parachute to inflate, a lot of altitude could be lost, reducing the model's duration in the air as it falls quickly to the ground.

For this experiment, you should perform drop tests in which you find out how long it takes for a parachute to open when blown out of a tube. Different folding techniques will affect how soon the parachute fully opens. You should try different size parachutes and different size tubes to see if they have any effect on the opening rate and your folding technique.

### Where to Start:

The book *Model Rocket Design & Construction* describes how to determine the size of a parachute for a desired descent speed. You'll also want to look in your library for other books on parachutes and see what folding techniques these publications recommend.

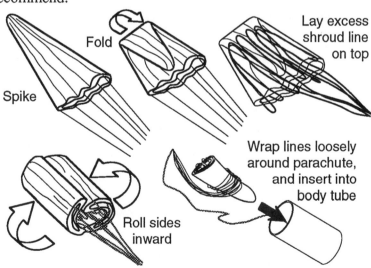

## Parachute Recovery Systems #7

**Project**: Determine the effect of solar heating on a parachute's descent rate.

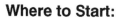

### Background:

The purpose of this experiment is to see if the color of a parachute affects the descent rate of the model.

Warm air has less density than cooler air. Because of this, it will rise higher into the air. The purpose of this experiment is to see if it is possible to use this principle to keep a parachute in the air longer. You need to determine if sunlight on a black parachute will heat the air beneath it. If it does, will the warm air tend to rise and slow the descent of the model?

### Where to Start:

The book *Model Rocket Design & Construction* describes how to determine the size of a parachute for a desired descent speed.

Black parachutes can be made out of black plastic sheet. A black trash can liner bag will make excellent parachute material.

## Parachute Recovery Systems #8

**Project**: Develop a parachute that does not sway as it descends.

### Background:

Many parachutes sway back-and-forth as they descend. This swaying, called *oscillation,* can cause problems for some delicate payloads. If the payload is swaying as it touches down on the ground, it could hit something very hard causing damage to the object being carried. Other payloads, such as cameras need to be held fairly stable so that the pictures are not blurred.

The purpose of this experiment is to develop a parachute that doesn't sway very much, and still falls slow enough that the payload isn't damaged from fast and hard landings.

## Where to Start:

The book *Model Rocket Design & Construction* describes how to determine the size of a parachute for a desired descent speed. You'll also want to look in your library for other books on parachutes.

Apogee Components' *Technical Publication #3 — Increasing the Descent Time of Rocket Parachutes* may give you some ideas of where to start in creating your improved parachute.

Some ideas you could experiment with are: spill holes in the canopy, canopies made out of very porous cloth, shaped canopies, spinning parachutes, clusters of parachutes, and gliding parachutes.

Rocket Experiment

## 12

## Rocket Recovery #1

**Project**: Determine the type and color of tracking powder that works best for spotting rockets in the sky.

## Background:

Tracking powder is used in rockets that fly to extremely high altitudes. It is a powdery substance that creates a large puffy cloud in the sky to help you see the model's location.

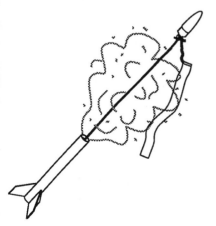

The purpose of this experiment is to find out what type of substance works best to help you see the model. What color works best? Should you use a different color when the sky is cloudy or hazy? What density or amount of tracking powder should be used? How does adding powder in the tube affect the way a parachute or streamer opens? Should the tracking powder be placed in some type of container or pouch so that it is easy to load into the model?

## Where to Start:

Try flying your rocket with different types of substances. Some powders that have been used in the past are: talcum powder, ground chalk, and tempera paint. Do not use a material that could burn easily, as this would be against the NAR safety code.

Fly your rockets in different weather conditions too - blue sky vs. cloudy days, and calm days vs. windy days, cold days vs. hot, humid days, etc.

**Rocket Experiment**

# 13

## Rocket Recovery #2

**Project**: Determine the dispersion pattern of models.

## Background:

The purpose of this experiment is to see how often a rocket will land at the same spot when repeatedly launched at same angle. The sum of all the landing locations would be called the *dispersion pattern*. Based on this pattern, what would be the odds of the rocket landing at exact same spot on the field for any given launch?

## Where to Start:

This project ties the mathematical subject of *statistics* with model rocketry, so you will want to start with a mathematics book that covers the theories of statistics and laws of probability. When flying your models, you will want to create target on the ground and try to get your models to land on that spot. You will then measure the distance and direction from the target spot each rocket hits. From multiple launches, you will get a "dart board" pattern of concentric rings. Using a statistics book, what would be the probability of hitting the target or landing in one of the concentric rings?

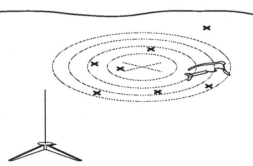

## Rocket Recovery #3

Rocket Experiment 14

**Project**: Create various techniques for precision duration contest events.

## Background:

The "precision duration" contest event has an objective of having your model take off and touch down as close as possible to a set "time limit." This *time limit* is selected at random, so you don't know before the day of the launch what the targeted duration time will be.

The intent of this experiment is to develop techniques for achieving precision time duration flights. For example, would you use the same model for a flight that must stay aloft for two minutes as you would for a one minute flight? What parameters would you vary?

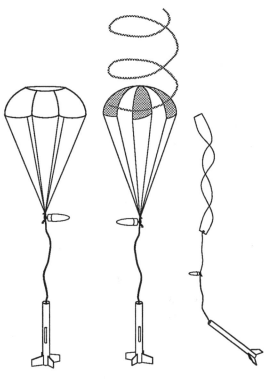

## Where to Start:

Research for this project might begin with you asking other modelers how they would fly this contest event. The best areas to reach modelers with this type of expertise is on a computer network such as the Internet's Rec.Models.Rockets newsgroup, or in the Rocketry forum on Comuserve Information Service.

Here are some of the parameters that affect how long the rocket will fly in the air: size of the model, weight of the model, type of motor used, the motor's delay time length, type of recovery device used (parachute, streamer, "X" form parachute), and launch angle. Develop some type of chart to help choose what type of model should be flown for durations of various time lengths.

**Rocket Experiment**

# 15

## Helicopter Recovery Systems #1

**Project**: Find the correlation between rotor blade length and the model's descent velocity.

## Background:

Helicopter models are unique among all model rockets. They lift-off like a regular rocket, and then transform mid-air — deploying rotor blades — which causes the model to spin down like a helicopter. Very little is known about how the rate of descent of these model rockets are determined.

In this science fair project, you need to find out how changing the length of the rotor blades affects the rate a which the model descends. Additionally, the model will spin at a certain rate; but does this rate change when the blades are lengthened?

Also consider the damage to the model when it lands on the ground. Long blades are more easily damaged on landing. What should be the maximum length of the blades (expressed as a ratio to the weight and size of the model)?

## Where to Start:

The book, *Model Rocket Design & Construction* has a section on helicopter recovery models. It shows how a model can be constructed so that it spins in flight.

You'll also want to contact some members of the National Association of Rocketry to find rare technical documents on the subject of helicopter models.

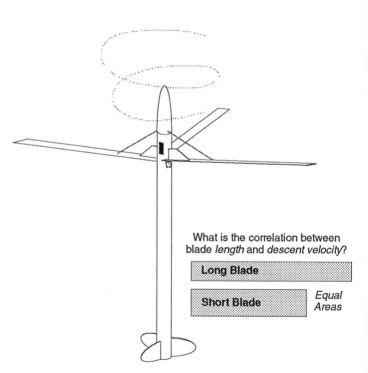

What is the correlation between blade *length* and *descent velocity?*

Long Blade

Short Blade | Equal Areas

**Rocket Experiment**

# 16

## Helicopter Recovery Systems #2

**Project**: Find the correlation between rotor blade *area* and a helicopter model's descent velocity.

## Background:

Helicopter models are unique among all model rockets. They lift-off like a regular rocket, and then transform mid-air — deploying rotor blades — which causes the model to spin down like a helicopter. Very little is known about how the rate of descent of these model rockets are determined.

In this project, you need to find out how changing the area of the rotor blades affects the rate a which the model descends. Will a wider blade fall slower than a narrower one with the same length? Additionally, the model will spin at a certain rate; but does this rate change when the blades are made wider?

## Where to Start:

The book *Model Rocket Design & Construction* has a section on helicopter recovery models. It shows how a model can be constructed so that it spins in flight.

You'll also want to contact some members of the National Association of Rocketry to find obscure technical documents on the subject of helicopter models.

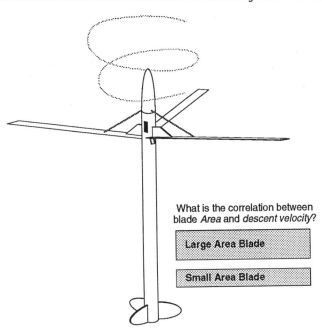

What is the correlation between blade *Area* and *descent velocity*?

Large Area Blade

Small Area Blade

**Rocket Experiment**

# 17

## Helicopter Recovery Systems #3

**Project**: Find the correlation between model mass and the model's descent velocity.

## Background:

Very little is known about how the descent rate of helicopter model rockets is determined. Helicopter models are unique among all model rockets. They lift-off like a regular rocket, and then transform mid-air — deploying rotor blades — which causes the model to spin down like a helicopter.

In this project, you need to find the relationship between the model's mass (with the same rotor blade size and area) and the rate a which the model descends. Mass can be easily added to the model by putting adding more wieght to the nose cone of the rocket. You can use clay for plastic nose cones, or metal washers to balsa wood nose cones.

Knowing the maximum weight of the model for a given blades size is basic information that can be used to establish design criteria for safe models that land without damage. Additionally, the model will spin at a certain rate; but how does this rate change when the model is made heavier?

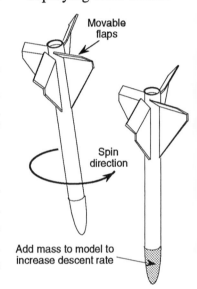

Movable flaps

Spin direction

Add mass to model to increase descent rate

## Where to Start:

The book *Model Rocket Design & Construction* has a section on helicopter recovery models. It shows how a model can be constructed so that it spins in flight.

You'll also want to contact some members of the National Association of Rocketry to find rare technical documents on the subject of helicopter models.

## Helicopter Recovery Systems #4

**Project**: Create a helicopter that has "flop" rotors which can be unfolded to help the model descend at a slower rate.

## Background:

Very little is known about how the descent rate of helicopter model rockets is determined. Helicopter models are unique among all model rockets. They lift-off like a regular rocket, and then transform mid-air — deploying rotor blades — which causes the model to spin down like a helicopter.

In this project, you need to develop a helicopter that has "flop rotors" which can be unfolded during the flight. The advantage would be a larger blade area that would help decrease the descent rate of the model so it

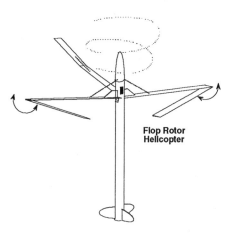

Flop Rotor
Helicopter

would stay in the air for a longer period of time. In addition, by folding the blades the model could be made smaller and thus, could fly higher in the air because of reduced drag.

## Where to Start:

The book *Model Rocket Design & Construction* has a section on helicopter recovery models. It shows how a model can be constructed so that it spins in flight.

You'll also want to contact some members of the National Association of Rocketry to find rare technical documents on the subject of helicopter models.

## Glider Design

**Project**: Determine the causes and the cure for spiral instability in gliders.

## Background:

Rocket launched gliders are popular with model rocketeers, because they take

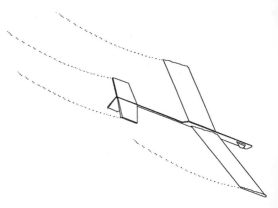

off like a rocket and then glide down like an airplane. But many gliders spiral down to the ground quickly after rocket motor burnout instead of transitioning into a level glide. The intent of this project is to identify the factors that contribute to this problem, and to solutions that can be used to correct it.

## Where to Start:

The book *Model Rocket Design & Construction* has a section on glider recovery models. This will give you a start in building glider models.

You'll also want to search your library for books about model airplanes, and glider trimming techniques. One publication you might consider is Apogee Components' Technical Publication #8, entitled: *"Glider Trimming."*

**Rocket Experiment**

**20**

## Glider Pod Design #1

**Project**: Determine glider pod pylon offset distance for front engine boost gliders.

## Background:

Rocket launched gliders are popular with model rocketeers because they take off like a rocket and then glide down like an airplane. Because they take off under rocket power, it is important that they fly straight so they don't create a safety hazard by looping around dangerously. Achieving stability during boost is hard with gliders because of the wing tries to make the glider pitch up (flip over on its back) as it climbs upward. The faster the model flies, the more it wants to pitch upward. To counteract this, the rocket motor is mounted on a pylon at a distance above the wing. This creates a downward force. When the

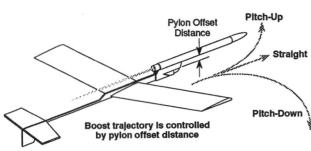

Pylon Offset Distance · Pitch-Up · Straight · Pitch-Down

Boost trajectory is controlled by pylon offset distance

forces balance out, the model will boost perfectly straight.

A pylon distance too high will cause the model to pitch down, while a pylon too short will not be sufficient to keep the model from pitching upward. Compounding the problem, different thrust motors will make the rocket boost at different speeds, which affects the lift force created by the wing; increasing or decreasing the pitching tendency of the model.

The intent of this research project is to find out what the offset distance the motor pylon should be set at (for a given area). How does this height change for different thrust rocket motors? Does the length of the pod also affect the trajectory?

## Where to Start:

The book *Model Rocket Design & Construction* has a section on glider recovery models. This will give you a starting point for building glider models. This book is available from Apogee Components.

**Rocket Experiment**

## 21 Glider Pod Design #2

**Project**: Create a device to prevent the recovery sytem from getting tangled with a glider.

## Background:

Rocket launched gliders are popular with model rocketeers because they take off like a rocket and then glide down like an airplane. One problem that occurs often with front engine gliders is that they occasionally get tangled with the recovery device on the

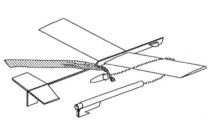

motor pod. This situation is called a *"red baron"* by modelers.

The purpose of this experiment would be to create a device or method of preventing the recovery system (streamer or parachute) for the motor pod from getting tangled up with the glider when the pod falls off the model.

## Where to Start:

The book *Model Rocket Design & Construction* has a section on glider recovery models. This will give you a start in building glider models that boost straight and fly well.

Rocket
Experiment

# 22

## Rocket Fin Design #1

**Project**: Determine the best criteria for fin design to prevent fin flutter.

## Background:

Very thin fins will begin to vibrate when the model flies very fast. This is called *"flutter."* Sometimes the flutter is so bad that it causes the fins to fall off during the flight. Even when flutter is not too bad, it still creates drag; which then robs from the maximum altitude the model could achieve.

This project would be to find out what criteria could be used to design fins that resist fluttering. Typically flutter occurs with high fin "span-to-chord" length ratios. But what other factors contribute to flutter?

First, determine a way to detect that the flutter problem is occurring. This might be through measuring the model's altitude, or by listening for the buzzing sound that sometimes occurs with fluttering fins. You'll probably want to use a fairly flexible material (such as thin cardboard) so that you can make sure that it does occur on your model. Then start to devise a way of preventing it from happening.

## Where to Start:

The book *Model Rocket Design & Construction* has basic guidelines on sizing fins to make the rocket stable. It also includes a number of ways to strengthen fins and attaching them to models.

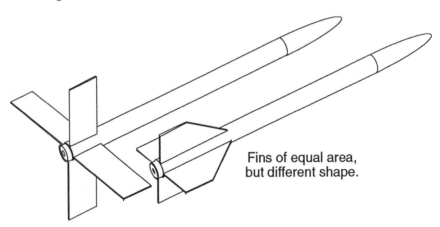

Fins of equal area, but different shape.

## Rocket Fin Design #2

**Project**: Determine how the altitude of a rocket is affected by the rate of spin of a model.

### Background:

It is well known that a spinning rocket does not travel as high as a non-spinning one. This is because it takes energy to make the rocket spin, which must be robbed from the kinetic energy of the fast moving rocket. Because there is less kinetic energy, it will not be able to fly as high. But what is the correlation between spin rate and the altitude achieved by the rocket?

In this experiment, you will force a rocket to spin and then track it to see how high it flies. Determining the spin rate of the model will also need to be determined. It might be possible to video tape the launch, and then review it in slow motion to count the number of times the model spins per second. You should paint one fin on the model a different color to make it easier to detect spinning.

You should then begin to change the rate at which the rocket spins, and see how this affects the models altitude.

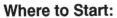

### Where to Start:

The book *Model Rocket Design & Construction* has basic guidelines on sizing fins to make the rocket stable. It also includes a number of ways to induce a spin into the rocket in a safe manner.

## Rocket Fin Design #3

**Project**: Define the stability laws for models with a "ring" fin.

### Background:

A *"ring"* finned rocket has a tube of larger diameter arranged concentrically around the body tube of the rocket. These types of models are very stable when they lift off. However, there are no available rules modelers can use to design these different looking fins successfully. Ring fins that are too large will have more drag, and therefore these models will not be able to fly as high as possible.

The intent of this experiment is to find out the minimum size ring fin that can be used that will still allow the model to be stable when flown. What should the diameter of the ring fin be, compared to the diameter of the body tube of the rocket? How long should it be? Where should the furthest aft location of the rocket's CG be for the model to fly stable? Any rules that you come up with should be "generalized;" that is, they should be based on ratios of tube diameters, and not on a specific size tube.

## Where to Start:

The book *Model Rocket Design & Construction* has basic guidelines on sizing fins to make the rocket stable. This might help you to create a stable flying rocket using ring fins.

Ring Fin

### Rocket Experiment

## 25  Rocket Liftoff Velocities

**Project**: Determine any increase in liftoff velocity gained by using a piston launcher.

## Background:

A piston launcher is a device used to increase the pressure beneath the base of a rocket motor at liftoff using the gases produced by the burning rocket motor. This increase in pressure kicks the model into the air, like a shell being blasted from a cannon. Modelers who compete in rocket competitions regularly use a piston launcher to help boost the model to higher altitudes.

The intent of this project is to measure the velocity of a rocket as it leaves the piston and compare it to that of a model leaving a launch rod or tower.

An additional comparison of the time from motor ignition to the point where the rocket passes a certain height should also be compared. This is to see if there is any delay created by the piston launcher when it hits its "stop." This might slow the model down slightly as it lifts off.

To measure this velocity accurately, you will need a fast and accurate timing device. This could be a beam of light that is broken by the passage

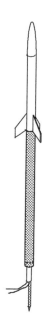

of a rocket fin traveling through it. See Experiment #31 for a description of this system and wher you might obtain some supplies.

## Where to Start:

The book *Model Rocket Design & Construction* has basic guidelines for developing a piston launcher. Also, contact some members of the National Association of Rocketry to find out more information about piston launchers, and for help in creating the electronic timing devices necessary to make accurate readings.

**Rocket Experiment**

# 26

## Rocket Liftoff Forces #1

**Project**: Determine any forces acting on a rocket as it leaves a launch rod.

## Background:

The long thin rod from which a rocket is launched is flexible and often bends when the rocket is launched. If this occurs just as the rocket leaves the top of the rod, the whipping effect could cause the model to change direction. As you can imagine, this is a very dangerous situation.

When the launch rod flexes, it will try to return to its original position (like a spring) and can be easily seen as a whipping action.

This flexing of the rod is caused by forces which can be measured. You may need to use a video camera to document the events at liftoff, because they happen so fast. It may then be possible to measure how far the launch rod flexed, and therefore determine the amount of force required to make it bend. The illustration on the next page shows how this force can be determined from the amount that the rod deflects.

The intent of this experiment is to see how much whipping occurs at liftoff. This topic can be further explored by changing the angle at which the model is aimed, and by varying the mass of the rocket.

Tip-off

## Where to Start:

Look in your library for "material properties" books. These engineering books will contain tables or charts that you can use to determine the forces on the bending rod (once you know how far it has flexed). You'll need them if you use a rod made from another material besides aluminum or stainless steel.

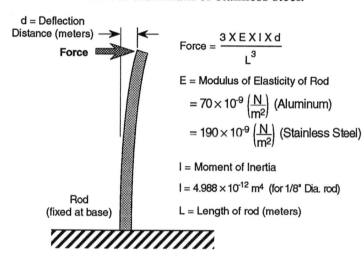

d = Deflection Distance (meters)

**Force**

Rod (fixed at base)

$$Force = \frac{3 \times E \times I \times d}{L^3}$$

E = Modulus of Elasticity of Rod

$$= 70 \times 10^{-9} \left(\frac{N}{m^2}\right) \text{ (Aluminum)}$$

$$= 190 \times 10^{-9} \left(\frac{N}{m^2}\right) \text{ (Stainless Steel)}$$

I = Moment of Inertia

$I = 4.988 \times 10^{-12} \, m^4$ (for 1/8" Dia. rod)

L = Length of rod (meters)

Rocket Experiment

**27**

## Rocket Liftoff Forces #2

**Project**: Determine any forces created by the wind acting on a rocket as it leaves a launch rod.

## Background:

This experiment is similar to experiment #26 listed above, except you will try to determine what effects wind plays in causing launch rod whip.

Rocket Experiment

**28**

## Rocket Aerodynamics #1

**Project**: Determine the effectiveness of turbulators on decreasing the drag on blunt shaped rockets.

## Background:

In classical aerodynamics, the lowest drag for a rocket occurs when the shape of the rocket is well streamlined (long teardrop shape). Some models cannot use this principle, because they have a very large, blunt shaped nose cone, and overall,

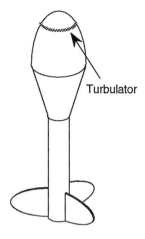

Turbulator

they are fairly short in length.

Turbulators are used in situations where airflow separates from the surface of an object moving through the air. When the airflow separates from the object, it creates higher drag than it would if it remained attached. A turbulator tries to prevent this extra drag by causing the air to become turbulent so that it will remain attached to the surface of the model.

Turbulators are best used when airflow travels around sharp corners on the back side of an object. Turbulent air turns corners easier than laminar flow air, so it doesn't become detached from the surface, and hence the drag does not increase as much.

The intent of this project is to see if turbulators placed near the front of a blunt shaped rocket can reduce the drag of a short, blunt rocket. A turbulator can be made with a thick piece of tape, so that it can be removed or repositioned as necessary. The experimental proceedure is to launch the same model with and without the turbulator and measure the altitude of each to see if the turbulator helped reduce drag on the rocket. A wind tunnel investigation can also be used to take accurate measurements of the drag force on the model.

**Where to Start:**

Look in your library for aircraft aerodynamics books. These engineering books will explain more fully the differences between laminar and turbulent flow, and how a turbulator is best used, and where it should be placed on the model.

Rocket Experiment

**29**

**Rocket Aerodynamics #2**

**Project**: Determine a method to measure base drag of a model rocket.

**Background:**

One of the factors that determines how high a rocket will fly is the amount of *'base drag'* is produced by the model. Base drag is just one component of the overall drag of the rocket (profile drag, induced drag, skin friction drag, etc.). The intent of this experiment is to determine a way to measure the component of base drag of the rocket. You will also need to determine how the base drag changes when the motor is thrusting.

This would be a good experiment for those individuals that have access to a wind tunnel.

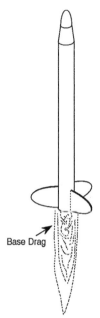

**Base Drag**

### Where to Start:

Look in your library for aircraft aerodynamics books. These books should explain better the drag theory, and how it affects the performance of a rocket.

Also try to find the book: *"Advanced Topics in Model Rocketry,"* by Gordon K. Mandell, George J. Caporaso, and William P. Bengen. MIT Press, 1973. ISBN 0-262-02096-3. This book has an excellent chapter covering drag on a model rocket. If you cannot get it through your local library, write to the National Association of Rocketry Technical Service (NARTS). Their address is listed in Appendix A at the end of this book.

Rocket Experiment **30**

## Rocket Aerodynamics #3

**Project**: Investigate "cone" shaped rockets

### Background:

Cone shaped rockets are unique among all models, because they don't require fins to stabilize them during flight. As long as the center-of-gravity of the model is in the correct place, the cone shaped model will fly straight.

The intent of this experiment is to determine the best cone angle of the model for achieving the highest altitudes. You should also determine the relationship between the "cone angle" and the drag coefficient ($C_d$) of the model.

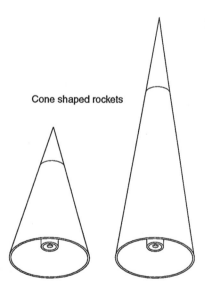

Cone shaped rockets

### Where to Start:

Start with the book *"Model Rocket Design and Construction."* The stability section of this book shows the correct relationship between the length of the cone and where you should position the center-of-gravity of the model.

It is possible to determine the $C_d$ of the model by tracking it to apogee (highest point in the flight), and then using a computer program to find out what the $C_d$ of the model was to reach this height. Read the section in this book called *Coefficient of Drag Estimation from Altitude Measurements* to find out how to use this technique.

### Rocket Experiment 31

## Rocket Ejection Charges

**Project**: Measure the strength of ejection charges from various rocket motors

### Background:

The ejection charge is one of the components built into a model rocket motor. When the ejection charge fires, it pressurizes the inside of the rocket tube to force the nose cone and parachute out of the model. If the volume inside the tube is too large and/or ejection charge is weak, the parachute may be never pushed out of the rocket.

The intent of this test is to measure the pressure created by the ejection charge and compare it to the internal volume of the rocket body tube. This test can be duplicated for motors from various manufacturers.

The pressure in the tube may be found by the process of "reverse engineering." If you could determine the velocity (hence acceleration) that the nose cone departs the rocket body, you could work backward using Newton's third law (**F=ma**) to find the force it took to move the nose cone (with a mass of "m"). This force will be a result of the pressure of the gases produced by the ejection charge, and the base area of the nose cone (**Pressure = F/Area**).

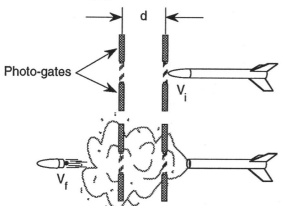

Here are the formulas used to find the pressure inside the model using a set-up shown in the illustration. This method requires determining the velocity of the nose cone as it leaves the body tube. An accurate timing device and photogates (infared photo sensors similar to the ones used at some stores to let the owner know when someone has walked into the store) to start and stop the timer are necessary to find this velocity.

$$v_f = \frac{\text{distance between Photogates}}{\text{time}}$$

$$\text{Acceleration of nose cone} = \frac{v_f - v_i}{\text{Time it takes for nose cone to reach } v_f}$$

Note: $v_f$ is reached when the nose cone leaves the tube. So if you set up the photogates to start when the nose cone just starts to move, and then stop when the shoulder of the nose cone exits the tube, this would be used to calculated the acceleration of the nose cone. From the illustration, "d" — the distance between photogates — should be equal to the length of the nose cone shoulder.

$$F_{(\text{required to move nosecone})} = m_{(\text{nose cone})} \times \text{acceleration}_{(\text{nose cone})}$$

$$\text{Pressure}_{(\text{inside tube})} = \frac{F_{(\text{required to move nosecone})}}{\text{Area of nose cone base}}$$

Once this pressure is known, the experiment can be repeated with a larger volume tube to see how the change in pressure affects the acceleration of the nose cone. Finally, a parachute could be inserted into the tube to see what changes (if any) this makes in the experiment.

## Where to Start:

Look in your library for books on physics and measuring accelerations. You might also perform this experiment using a "ballistics" approach and use momentum change to find the force of the ejection charge. This second approach is not as accurate, but it does not require any expensive electronic equipment to make the measurements. Contact Apogee Components if you can not find information on using this technique to determine the velocity at which the nose cone exits the model.

A company that sells photo-gates is:
PASCO Scientific
P.O. Box 619011
Roseville, CA 95678-9011

**Rocket Experiment**

**32**

## Strength of Balsa Wood

**Project**: Measure the strength of balsa wood and how that is affected by various reinforcement methods.

## Background:

Balsa wood is used in model rocketry because it has a high strength-to-weight ratio. The intent of this experiment is to measure the bending strength of balsa wood of various densities and of different grades (i.e., "A" grain, "B" grain or "C" grain). From this, a recommendation can be made for selection of balsa wood to be used for fins on various size model rockets.

An easy strength test is to make a simple beam from the balsa wood, and

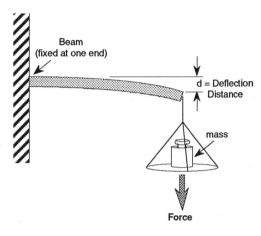

load one end with weights and see how much it deflects. You'll also want to find out how much weight the beam can hold before it breaks.

All the test samples for this type of experiment must be exactly the same size and length for any comparable results to be obtained.

Once the basic strength of the wood is known, various methods of strengthening it can be tried and evaluated.

## Where to Start:

Look in your library for books listing strength of materials to see how a test could be performed. These books will have charts to show how much force is needed to make a beam bend (deflect). An example of this was shown in experiment #26. Also talk to your local hobby shop owner to find out about how balsa wood is classified according to its density and grain orientation.

The book *Model Rocket Design & Construction* show various ways that balsa fins are typically strengthened. You might find it useful in getting some ideas on how strong fins are made.

**Rocket Experiment 33**

## Strength of Body Tubes

**Project**: Measure the strength of body tubes.

## Background:

Nearly all body tubes are made from kraft paper, which are wound in a spiral fashion. But is this the best method to make a strong tube? Can tubes be made out of other types of paper and wound in a different way to make them stronger?

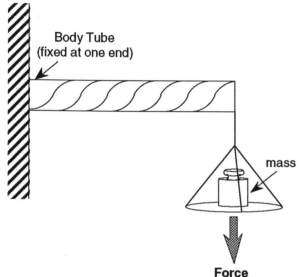

Body Tube (fixed at one end)

mass

Force

Because we are also interested in keeping the weight of the rocket low, which method will yield the highest strength per weight of the tube?

An easy strength test can be perform by making a simple beam from the tube as shown in the illustration. You then suspend weights from the free end and see how much it deflects, and/or how much weight it can hold before it kinks.

All the test samples for this type of experiment must be exactly the same size and length, so that comparable results can be obtained. You only want to test the material used, and how the tube is assembled. *{Obviously, a larger diameter tube will be stronger than a skinnier one}*. After you test the tubes for maximum strength, you will also want to weigh them to find out the the strength-to-weight ratio of each tube.

## Where to Start:

The illustration shows one way to perform a strength test. You could also stand the tube on its end and pile weight on top to see how much the tube can hold before it buckles and collapses. This would be called a *compression test.*

Look in the library for books listing strengths of materials to see how a test can be performed. These books will have charts to show how much force is needed to make a beam bend (deflect). An example of this was shown in Experiment #26.

## Decreasing Damage to Body Tubes

**Project**: Find out how the length of the shock cord affects damage to the tube from nose cone "snap-back."

## Background:

Body tubes are often damaged at the top end when the parachute ejects. When the recovery system ejects, the elastic shock cord stretches out completely, and then springs back — the nose cone sometimes hitting the tube and deforming the end or ripping the tube (creating a "zipper effect" tube).

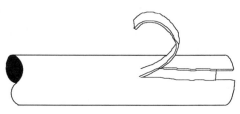

"Zippered" body tube caused by nosecone snap-back

The purpose of this experiment would be to vary the length of the shock cord to see what is the minimum length the cord can be used without damaging the end of the tube.

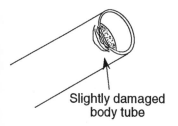

Slightly damaged body tube

Many shock cords are made from 1/8" wide sewing elastic. But is this the best material? What about cords that aren't stretchable (such as kevlar or thin, flexible wire cable)? Do these "non-stretchable" cords cause other types of damage? Are they prone to causing damage elsewhere on the model?

## Where to Start:

This is an experiment that can be easily be done without launching the model into the air. If you strapped the model down to the launch pad (by taping it securely to the launch pad), it will not fly into the air when the motor is ignited. Then you could view (and possibly videotape) what happens when the nose cone ejects from the model. From this, you could make easier and better conclusions without having to worry about recovering the model after each launch. But you will want to perform some actual flights to see if the results in the air are comparible to the results on the ground. Also try varying the launch angle of the pad. Does this effect the type or amount of damage?

## Timing Devices

**Project**: Develop a simple, lightweight timer.

### Background:

There is a big need in model rocketry for a simple lightweight timing device. Such a device would trigger some type of action at a predetermined time in the rocket's flight. Such an action might be to release the parachute after a delay of several seconds following the ejection charge of the model. This would let the model descend lower to the ground before the parachute opens, thereby reducing the drift of the model. The uses for such a timer are explained in Exp. #8 and #40.

To be useful in smaller model rockets, the criteria for the timer is: small size (1 cm in diameter) and low mass (less than 5 grams). It could be mechanical or electrical, but it must be accurate to within ± 1 second and be initiated (started) by the ejection charge of the model.

## Airspeed Measurement

**Project**: Develop a simple airspeed measurement system.

### Background:

It is possible to measure many of the flight parameters of a rocket. One interesting parameter is the speed of the rocket. The intent of this experiment is to develop an instrument or procedure to measure this velocity, and also possibly measure the acceleration of the model.

### Where to Start:

Start by reading the beginning of this book under the heading of *"Measuring Velocity and Acceleration."* It will tell you some simple ways to measure these two parmeters.

Be sure to look in your library for books on aircraft instrumentation. Also contact other rocketeers (on the INTERNET in the newsgroup Rec.Models.Rockets, or through the National Association of Rocketry) for information about this subject.

**Free-Fall Tests**

**Project**: Use a rocket to drop objects to measure their aerodynamic parameters.

## Background:

With model rockets, objects can be lofted to extremely high altitudes. Using this fact, it is possible to drop these objects from a rocket and subject them to zero gravity experiments, and/or to measure aerodynamic properties such as their drag coefficients.

For example, ping-pong balls can be dropped and their descent rate timed so that a drag coefficient can be measured. The ping-pong ball also makes a great drop payload because they don't present any safety hazard.

## Where to Start:

Start by reading the beginning of this book under the subject of *"Measuring Velocity and Acceleration"* of the model. It would be possible to use these techniques to determine how fast the object is falling.

Once the decent rate is known, you can use the "terminal velocity" equation to find out the coefficient of drag of the falling object. This equation is:

$$C_d = \frac{2\,g\,m}{\rho\,S\,v^2}$$

Test Object
being dropped

Where:  $g = 9.81$ m/s$^2$ (acceleration due to gravity)
$m$ = mass of object in grams
$\rho$ = density of air (1225 g/m$^3$)
$S$ = Frontal area of object (m$^2$)
$v$ = maximum velocity of the falling object (m/s)

**Rocket Experiment**

# 38

## Piston Launchers and Optimum Mass

**Project**: Determine the effects of using a piston launcher on the optimum mass of a model.

## Background:

There is a "best" mass of a rocket that will allow the model to travel to its highest potential for each different type of rocket motor. This is called the "optimum" mass for the model. A rocket that is too heavy will not fly as high as a lighter weight one. This is easy to demonstrate and is also logical to most modelers (a simple example of this is a person throwing a softball versus throwing a metal shot-put). But if the model is too light, it will also not travel to its maximum potential altitude. An example of this is a person throwing a ping-pong ball versus a smooth golf ball. The heavier ball will travel a lot farther, because it weighs more.

So somewhere between "too heavy" and "too light" is the *optimum* mass of the model. This mass is best found by running computer simulations to find out how heavy the model should be to fly highest.

A piston launcher is a device used to increase the pressure beneath the base of a rocket motor at liftoff utilizing the gases produced by the burning rocket motor. This increase in pressure kicks the model into the air, like a shell being blasted from a cannon. Modelers who compete in rocket competition regularly use a piston launcher to help boost the model to higher altitudes.

With computer simulations, it is easy to determine the optimum mass of a model. But these simulations assume that the lift-off velocity of the model isn't being aided by the piston launcher. So these simulations won't accurately predict the final velocity of the model using a piston launcher.

The intent of this experiment is to find out how the optimum mass of the model changes with the use of a piston launcher. To find this out, you will need to determine the how the height of the model changes when launched from a piston launcher and how this altitude changes when mass is added or removed from the model. To make this comparison, you'll will also have to find out how high the model will fly when launched in the standard way (without the piston launcher).

## Where to Start:

The optimum mass for any particular motor can be found by running computer simulations to find out how heavy the model should be to fly the highest. Computer software that predicts the altitude of a model can be found from several manufacturers. Look in the latest issue of *High Power Rocketry* or *Sport Rocketry* to find such manufacturers. If you can't find any, contact Apogee Components, which sells this type of software too.

When doing flight demonstrations, choose a "mini" or "micro" rocket motors. These have lower weight paper cases. The larger, "regular" size rocket motors, have extremely heavy paper cases. Most of these "regular" rocket motors weigh so much, that it is nearly impossible to build a rocket around them that isn't already over the optimum mass. Even by choosing a smaller motor, you will still have to be careful to build the model extremely light. You will want to show that a lower weight model doesn't fly as high as a heavier model. You can then add weight (in the form of tracking powder) to make it heavier when flying it again.

You should also read the section in this book that describes the various tracking techniques that you can use to determine how high your rocket flies. Once you track your various models, you can make a graph that displays the weight of the model versus its altitude (like the one shown on the previous page).

The book *Model Rocket Design & Construction* has basic guidelines developing a piston launcher. Also contact some members of the National Association of Rocketry to find out more information about building and using piston launchers. Also read Apogee's Technical Publication #11 - "Piston Launcher Plans."

**Rocket Experiment**

# 39

## Internal Pressure of Piston Launchers

**Project**: Determine the pressure inside a piston launcher when a model is launched.

### Background:

A piston launcher is a device used to increase the pressure beneath the base of a rocket motor at liftoff, using the gases produced by the burning rocket motor. This increase in pressure kicks the model into the air, like a shell being blasted from a cannon. Modelers who compete in rocket competitions regularly use a piston launcher to help boost the model to higher altitudes.

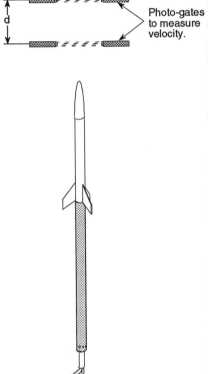

Photo-gates to measure velocity.

Most piston launchers are made from cardboard tubes, which sometimes split because of the high pressure inside the tube. This experiment would be to measure the pressure rise inside the piston launcher as the model rocket is ignited. By using this information, better piston launcher designs could be created to make them more efficient and durable.

### Where to Start:

The book *Model Rocket Design & Construction* has basic guidelines for developing a piston launcher. Also contact some members of the National Association of Rocketry to find out more information about piston launchers.

You might approach this experiment from one of two ways. The first would be to use electronic instrumentation to actually measure the pressure inside the piston launcher. The second would use a ballistics approach to find out the velocity of the model as the rocket leaves the piston. From this, you could do reverse engineering to find out what the pressure had to be inside the tube to kick the model off at this velocity. See Experiment #31 for hints on using this technique.

**Rocket Experiment**

**40**

## Boosted Dart Launch Velocity

**Project**: Determine the amount of speed a boosted dart gains when it is kicked off the top of its host launcher.

## Background:

A boosted dart is similar to a two stage rocket, but the top "stage" doesn't have a rocket motor in it. The bottom "stage" uses a conventional rocket motor with a delay charge, and not the "special" *booster* motor. This allows the model to coast to its highest altitude before ejecting the top "dart" stage. The dart is then kicked forward by the ejection charge of the lower stage so it can coast even higher upward. The lower stage utilizes rear ejection to deploy its own recovery device.

The dart is also more streamlined than the lower stage (the aft end comes to a point to minimize drag). Because it has lower drag, it can coast a lot further than the lower stage.

The intent of this experiment is to measure the velocity gained by a boosted dart as it is kicked off the booster section, and to calculate how high a dart is able to coast.

## Where to Start:

This project should probably be done with the lower stage strapped down to the launcher so that it can't lift off. When the motor is ignited, the entire model remains stationary. After the delay burns, the dart will be kicked into the air by the ejection charge.

You will want to measure the velocity of the model as it comes off the lower model. To measure this velocity accurately, you will need a fast and accurate timing device. This could be a beam of light that is broken by the passage of a rocket fin traveling through it and is called a "photogate." See experiment #31 for more info on using photogates to measure velocity.

Knowing the velocity of the dart, you could

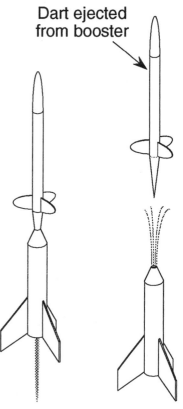

Dart ejected from booster

Dart at lift-off

use simple equations of motion to find out how high it will travel. Or, you could measure its peak altitude, and use the equations to find the velocity it had when it was kicked off the lower stage.

An actual boosted dart will need its own recovery system. This will require some type of timer to allow the dart to coast upward before deploying its recovery device. Creating this timer would make another excellent rocketry science fair project, and it is described in Experiment #35.

## Delayed Staging

**Project**: Determine if delaying the moment of "staging" will actually help a model boost higher into the sky.

## Background:

The advantage of staging a rocket is to achieve a high altitude. It achieves this advantage by having a very high burnout velocity of the top stage of the model. But high velocity means that the drag on the model will be higher - which will actually limit the altitude of the model.

Typically when staging, the upper stage ignites as soon as the lower stage burns out. But it is possible to delay the instant of staging by using a motor in the lower stage that has a short delay. This would allow the model to coast briefly and therefore slow down slightly

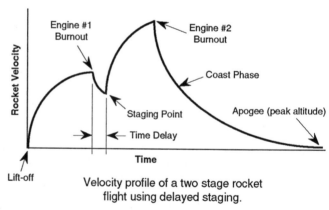

Velocity profile of a two stage rocket flight using delayed staging.

before the second stage ignites. Then the drag on the upper stage would be lower because it is flying slightly slower as the graph shows.

The purpose of this experiment would be to see how long of a delay should be used to gain maximum altitude.

## Where to Start:

This experiment can be run completely with computer simulations. Computer software that predicts the altitude of a model can be found from several manufacturers. Look in the latest issue of *High Power Rocketry* or *Sport Rocketry* magazine to find such manufacturers. If you can't find any, contact Apogee Components, which sells this type of software too.

The booklet, *Model Rocket Propulsion* from Apogee Components also tells more about the concepts of staging in general, and also of delayed staging.

It would also be possible to perform actual launches and find the maximum altitude by using optical tracking techniques. If you attempt the launch, it is important to recognize that motors with delays may not be able to ignite the upper stage. This is because the clay cap of the lower stage may clog the nozzle of the upper stage when it is blown out by the ejection charge. To lessen this problem, you should use the Apogee Components micro motors in this experiment. Read Apogee's *Technical Publication #6 - Staging Techniques for Apogee Rocket Motors*.

## Rocket Noise #1

**Project**: Record the noise level inside a rocket during the flight.

## Background:

The noise inside a model rocket can be important in experiments involving live biological payloads. If any change takes place in the "living" payload, you need to know if it was because of the forces of acceleration, or if it was reacting to the loud noise inside the rocket.

By recording the noise inside the rocket, you can test the "living" payload to see what response it makes as a result of the noise. This can be done while it is still on the ground by playing back the rocket "noise" to the living payload at the correct volume level, corresponding to the level recorded during an actual flight.

## Where to Start:

Thanks to modern electronics, it is possible to build a small "solid state" recording device. The sound is recorded on a integrated circuit chip, and can be played back at a later time. You may have seen inexpensive toys that use these devices. You can either use one of these toys, or you can build your own electronic recording device. Apogee Components also sells a recorder device too.

## Rocket Noise #2

**Project**: Make a rocket that generates a whistling sound.

### Background:

In studying sound wave propagation, it is first necessary to generate a sound wave that can be heard above the noise of the rocket motor. Although this can be done with electronic buzzers, it is more fun to generate a whistling sound from the rocket itself.

The whistling sound is created by air flowing over the rocket. This creates forces on the model. Sometimes, if a part is loose, it will begin to vibrate and make a buzzing noise. The faster the vibration, the higher the pitch whistling or buzzing sound that is generated.

Another way of generating a whistling sound is by having the air itself create a whistling sound. This concept is easily demonstrated with a toy whistle. When you blow air into it, the air interacts with the walls of the whistle, and sets up a sound wave that can be heard.

### Where to Start:

The two methods of generating noise with the rocket were listed above. You can experiment by mounting different things to the rocket to see which makes the loudest noise when the rocket is flown. Some things that vibrate are streched rubber bands and plastic ribbons.

To generate a whistle sound, you might try mounting various types of toy whistles to the side or nose cone of the rocket. Experiment until you find one that works best.

# Chapter 5

# Project Ideas: 26 *Demonstrations*

Demonstration projects are sometimes allowed in science fairs because they show that the student is gaining knowledge in the subject being studied. Even though no *new* information about the topic is being discovered, it still shows that an effort was made to gain information unknown to them.

These demonstration projects are often more easier to do than the experiments listed in the previous chapter. If you are running low on time to complete your science fair project, it is better to try one of these. But these projects can be also made more complex by trying to get more accurate data. In either case, these projects are a lot of fun to do. You may even find that a topic will give you an idea of your own. This is the best possible situation, so congratulate yourself!

Rocket Demo 1

## Rocket Mass versus Maximum Height

**Project**: Show the relationship between the rocket's weight and how high it is capable of flying.

### Where to Start:

This is a relatively simple project, and is great for younger children. You will select a single rocket, and use only the same type of rocket motors for each flight. Then the only difference between flights is the weight added to the rocket before it lifts off.

If you have a rocket that has a payload section, you can use simple weights like metal washers or small coins. Make sure that these objects are securely attached in the payload section so that they won't fall out. A penny falling from high in the air can cause injury if it hits someone.

For rockets without a payload section, you can

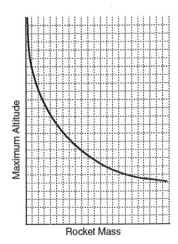

Maximum Altitude / Rocket Mass

use "tracking" powder to change the mass of the model. The more tracking powder added to the model, the heavier it will be. The added benefit is that the powder makes it easy to spot in the air - so determining altitude is much easier and more accurate.

Rocket Demo

**2**

## Distance Traveled versus Launch Angle

**Project**: Show the relationship between the how far a rocket travels, and the angle at which it was launched.

### Where to Start:

For this project, you first need to read the safety rules for model rocketry, which are located in the first chapter of this book. In these rules, you should never launch a rocket that is pointed greater than 30 degrees from straight up. But it is still possible to launch the rocket at a slight angle and see how far it lands from the launch pad.

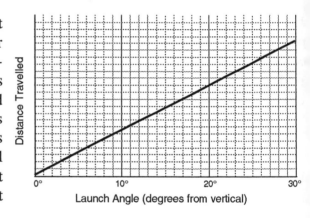

To get better results, only launch on a day with no wind. Any wind could cause your rocket to drift, making the results inaccurate. Also select a model that won't fly too high and that uses either tumble, featherweight, or helicopter recovery. Parachutes and streamers have a higher tendency to drift.

## The Operation of Model Rocket Motors

**Project**: Show how a model rocket motor works.

### Where to Start:

You will definitely want to read the booklet from Apogee Components called *"Model Rocket Propulsion."* This booklet explains how rocket motors work, and has many special sections which may interest you, such as: rocket performance prediction, staged models, and clustered-motor models. It also lists many different demonstration projects which might give you some other topics to explore with model rocket motors.

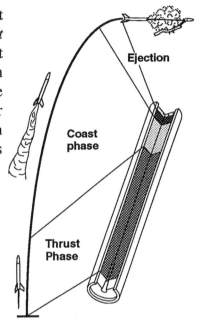

## Multi-Stage Rockets #1

**Project**: Show that a rocket using two rocket motors (staged together) is a good way to achieve ultra high altitudes.

### Where to Start:

Flying a two-stage rocket is a very easy project. You will want to demonstrate that two smaller motors can fly higher than a single motor that has a greater total power. This power rating is called the motor's *"Total Impulse."* For example, a "C" motor has twice the Total Impulse of a "B" motor; so it can be said that it also has twice the power.

For best results, the smaller motors (which are staged together) should have a smaller diameter than the bigger motor. The two stage rocket should be skinnier than the single stage rocket. *{Even though this adds another variable to the demonstration, it is one of the main advantages why staging is used in model rocketry.}*

If you use the 10.5 mm diameter Apogee rocket motors, you will want to also read *"Technical Publication #6 - Staging Techniques for Apogee Rocket Motors."* It describes the extra set-up procedures that these motors require.

You might also want to read the booklet from Apogee Components called *"Model Rocket Propulsion."* This booklet explains how rocket motors work, and has a special section on staged rockets. It may also give you some other topics to explore with model rocket motors.

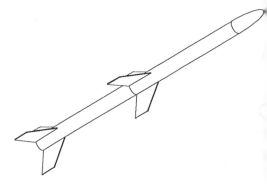

**Rocket Demo**

## Multi-Stage Rockets #2

**5**

**Project**: Demonstrate staging techniques to use when the motors are separated by long distances.

### Background:

Flying a two-stage rocket is a very easy project. It is easier and more reliable to stage rockets that are in direct contact with each other. But sometimes, you may want to have a long distance separating the two motors. In this case, the chances of the upper stage igniting are reduced. In this project, you will show the various methods that can be used to stage motors that are separated by long distances.

The project can be made more complete by finding out the furthest distance the motors can be separated and still be reliably ignited.

## Where to Start:

You will want to start your project by reading the chapter on multi-stage rockets in the book *"Model Rocket Design and Construction."* It tells you how to successfully stage motors that are not in direct contact. You want to also read *"Technical Publication #6 - Staging Techniques for Apogee Rocket Motors."* It describes the extra set-up requirements that these motors have, and how to use a special staging ignitor.

You might also want to read the booklet from Apogee Components called *"Model Rocket Propulsion."* This booklet explains how rocket motors work, and has a special section on staged rockets. It may also give you some other topics to explore with model rocket motors.

When launching your rockets, you can simplify the procedure by strapping the booster section down to the launch pad (i.e., tape it securely to the launch rod). Make sure that the upper stage has launch lugs so that it is guided by the launch rod when it ignites. This way, you can still test your staging methods, but the top stage of the model won't fly as high, so it will be easier to recover. Another benefit is that if the upper stage motor fails to ignite, the model will not come crashing down to the ground without a recovery device — it will just remain on the launch pad. *Safety Note: Do not approach the model while it is "operating" on the pad. Remain away from it until the flight is completely finished.*

Rocket Demo

**6**

## Clustered Rocket Motors

**Project**: Show that a rocket using two rocket motors (clustered together) is a good way to lift heavier rockets.

## Background:

Flying a cluster engine rocket is another easy project. You will want to demonstrate that two motors firing together can lift a heavier rocket than a single rocket motor.

All model rocket motors are designated by a power rating. This "power rating" is called the motor's *Total Impulse*. For example, a "C" motor has twice the Total Impulse of a "B" motor, so it can be said that it also has twice the power.

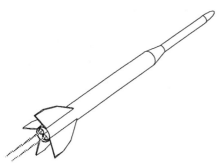

But the thrust force produced is not dependant on the power of the motor. For example, a "B2" motor has the same Total Impulse (power) as a "B8" motor, even though it has lower thrust. It is the "thrust" force produced that determines how heavy a rocket can be launched and still fly straight. Because it has more thrust, a "B8" can lift a heavier rocket than a "B2."

This demonstration can show that two small motors working together can even lift a heavier model than a rocket motor with more power. For example, two "A2" motors clustered together are capable of lifting a heavier rocket than a single "B2" motor.

## Where to Start:

If you use the 10.5 mm diameter Apogee rocket motors, you will want to also read *"Technical Publication #2 - Using Apogee High Performance Rocket Motors in Non-Apogee Kits"* Its chief use for this demonstration is that it contains a chart showing which motors can be used safely for lifting heavier rockets. When flying clustered rockets, do so only on a day with little or no wind.

You might also want to read the book *"Model Rocket Design and Construction,"* as it has a special section on cluster motor rockets.

Rocket Demo

**7**

## Rocket Motor Efficiency

**Project**: Show that a rocket with higher specific impulse can fly higher, and are therefore more efficient.

## Background:

In this demonstration, you want to find out what type of rocket motor is more efficient. This can be done by flying two different motors (of the same power rating) and seeing which one flies higher. The one that flies higher is then the most efficient at using the power available from the rocket motor.

This "power rating" that you will select is called the motor's *Total Impulse*. For example, a "C" motor has twice the Total Impulse of a "B" motor, so it can be said

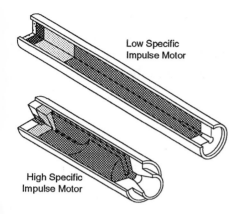

Low Specific
Impulse Motor

High Specific
Impulse Motor

that it also has twice the power.

For this demonstration, you will want to use two different motors that have the same "letter" in the motor's designation code. For example, you could use two different "B" motors.

The measure of efficiency that you are trying to show is this: "A motor with less propellant mass but the same Total Impulse as the other is more efficient."

## Where to Start:

You will want to start by reading the booklet from Apogee Components called *"Model Rocket Propulsion."* This booklet explains how rocket motors work, and has a special section on the different types of rocket motors, and how to calculate their efficiencies. This efficiency rating is called *"Specific Impulse,"* which is clearly explained in this excellent book. It may also give you some other topics to explore with model rocket motors.

Rocket
Demo

8

## Rocket Efficiency

**Project**: Show that a slower flying rocket is more efficient at flying through the atmosphere than a fast rocket.

## Background:

This project is different from the proceeding project in that you are testing the efficiency of a rocket in a different way. In the proceeding demonstration, the efficiency of the *propellant* used in the motor was rated. In this experiment, you are going to demonstrate that drag on a model affects the overall efficiency of the model, so that a slower flying rocket does indeed fly higher than a fast rocket.

In this demonstration, you will want to fly two motors of the same power but

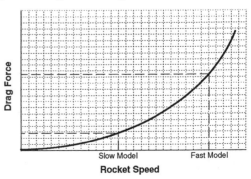

Rocket Speed

## Page 83

with different thrust levels. The "power rating" is called the motor's *Total Impulse*. For example, a "C" motor has twice the Total Impulse of a "B" motor, so it can be said that it also has twice the power. But it is the level of thrust that determines how fast the model will travel. This thrust level is designated by the first number (after the letter) on the motor. For example, a B2 motor has less thrust than a B6 motor. It will therefore take off slower than the B6.

As the illustration shows, the drag force experienced by a rocket increases as the model travels faster. The higher the drag force, the quicker the model will slow down when the motor stops thrusting. So it will not be able to coast as high after the motor burns out.

In this demonstration, you will show which thrust level makes the model fly higher, and what the optimum thrust level should be to obtain maximum altitude for a given weight of model rocket.

## Where to Start:

You will want to start by reading the booklet from Apogee Components called *"Model Rocket Propulsion."* This booklet explains how rocket motors work, and has a special section on the different types of rocket motors, and how to calculate which rocket will travel faster.

Also read *"Technical Publication #1 - Why Apogee Rocket Motors Make Models Fly Higher,"* which is also produced by Apogee Components. It will give you more background information about why some rocket motors travel higher than others.

Rocket Demo

# 9

**Methods of Fin Attachment**

**Project**: Show the various ways that fins can be attached to a model, and what can be done to make them stronger.

## Background:

A common problem that affects all beginning rocketeers is that the fins on their rockets come off easily when bumped. In this project, you will show the various methods of attaching the fins, and which types of glue work the best.

## Where to Start:

The book *"Model Rocket Design and Construction"* shows many different

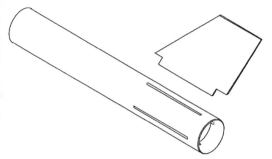

ways that fins can be attached to a model, and other ways they can be made stronger. It also lists which types of glue are used in rocketry and how they are best used. By knowing this information, you'll have a better idea about how to start this project.

Rocket
Demo

**10**

## Spin Stabilization

**Project**: Show that the trajectory of a rocket can be made straighter by spin stabilization.

### Background:

Making a model spin as it lifts-off causes an increase in angular momentum. Like a spinning top, the angular momentum helps keep the model pointed straight up; so it has a straighter trajectory.

You can also experiment with the rate at which the rocket spins, and see how this affects the straightness of the flight.

To make it easier to detect spinning, paint one fin of the model a different coler.

### Where to Start:

The book *"Model Rocket Design and Construction"* shows many different ways to induce spin into a model rocket. You can try each of these methods to see which works the best. Spinning models should also be compared against non-spinning rockets for straightness of trajectory, and maximum altitude attained.

## Rocket Motor Selection

**Project**: Show what the effects of *improper* motor selection can have on a model rocket's flight

## Background:

The purpose of this demonstration is to show what affect the length of the "delay" in rocket motor has on the flight of a model. You will fly the same rocket but with different delay lengths and see how high the rocket will be when the parachute is ejected.

For example, you could fly the same model with an A2-0, A2-3, A2-5, and an A2-7 rocket motor. Weigh the rocket before each flight to keep the weight the same for each flight, even if you are using the same model for all the flights. If necessary, you can add tracking powder to the low-weight models, to increase their mass. Then the only difference between flights is the delay length of the motors.

The demonstration could then be modified by angling the launch rod (so the flight is not straight up) and flying the various motors again. How does this change when the parachute is deployed. You might compare this to flights made on windy days when the model "weathercocks" into the wind. Would these flights be similar?

## Where to Start:

You will start by reading the booklet from Apogee Components called *"Model Rocket Propulsion."* This booklet explains how rocket motors work, and has a special section on selecting the right rocket motors for your models.

If you use the 10.5 mm diameter Apogee rocket motors (as listed in the above "background" section), you will want to also read *Technical Publication #2 - Using Apogee High Performance Rocket Motors in Non-Apogee Kits"* Its chief use for this demonstration is that it contains a chart showing which motors can be used safely for lifting heavier rockets. With its help, you can also predict what the trajectory of the rocket may look like with the motors you select.

You really need to build a strong model for this demonstration, because the "wrong" rocket motors will abuse the model. So start with the book *"Model Rocket Design and Construction"* which shows many different ways to make a model stronger and more durable. It also has a section on repairing any damage that might occur to your rocket.

Rocket
Demo

## 12

### Rocket Recovery Techniques #1

**Project**: Show the various recovery methods for bringing a rocket down.

## Background:

The are many methods of bringing down a rocket safely from the sky. These are: streamer recovery, parachute recovery, glider recovery, helicopter recovery, drag recovery, and flutter recovery.

The purpose of this project is to demonstrate how each of these methods work. You could also show when is the best time to use each type of recovery system — based on type of model, size, weight, motor used, wind conditions, etc.

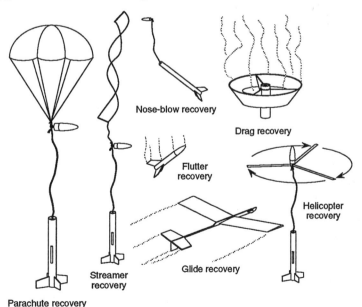

Nose-blow recovery

Drag recovery

Flutter recovery

Helicopter recovery

Streamer recovery

Glide recovery

Parachute recovery

## Where to Start:

The book *"Model Rocket Design and Construction"* describes each of these different recovery methods in full detail.

For this demonstration, you can build models for each technique and then videotape them for playback in your display. There are many kits that can be used to demonstrate the various techniques. However, building your own rockets to show the different recovery techniques will probably make a better exhibit.

Rocket Demo

# 13

## Rocket Recovery Techniques #2

**Project**: Show the effects of a spill hole in a parachute.

## Background:

A spill hole in a parachute allows air to flow through the chute at a faster rate. This has a few benefits to a modeler. First, it allows the parachute to fall faster, so that it doesn't drift too far during windy days. Second, it stabilizes the parachute so it doesn't sway back and forth.

The objective of this project is to show the benefits that a spill hole creates. To start, you will build your rocket and the parachute, launch it and record how it flies. Then you can cut a hole in the top of the chute and see how this affects its performance. You can then experiment to see what difference happens when the hole is enlarged.

To show the effect of a spill hole on stabilizing the parachute, you can shorten the lines on one side of the chute to cause it to sway. Then you can see how the hole decreases the swaying of the parachute.

Another method of bringing the model

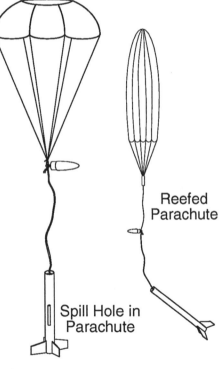

Reefed Parachute

Spill Hole in Parachute

down faster is by "reefing" the parachute shroud lines with a piece of tape (as shown in the illustration). You can fly you model this way, and compare it to a parachute with a spill hole in both descent velocity and by how much the model sways.

## Where to Start:

The book *"Model Rocket Design and Construction"* describes how to select the proper size parachute for your rocket.

*"Technical Publication #3 - Increasing the Descent Time of Rocket Parachutes"* from Apogee Components also has some information that you can use for this demonstration.

Rocket Demo **14**

## Piston Launchers

**Project**: Show that there is an altitude gain by using a piston launcher.

## Background:

A piston launcher is a device used to increase the pressure beneath the base of a rocket motor at liftoff, using the gases produced by the burning rocket motor. This increase in pressure kicks the model into the air, like a shell being blasted from a cannon. Modelers who compete in rocket competitions regularly use a piston launcher to help boost their models to higher altitudes.

The intent of this project is to show that a piston launcher can be used to increase the altitude of a model rocket. This can be done by launching the same model (with the same type of rocket motors) from a standard launch rod/pad, compared to when launched from a piston launcher. The altitude of the model would be tracked both times to see which method made the model fly higher.

If two identical models (same shape, weight and motors) where launched at the exact same time, you wouldn't need to measure the altitude of each rocket — you could just visually compare their performances to see which flies higher.

## Where to Start:

The book *Model Rocket Design & Construction* has basic guidelines developing a piston launcher. Also contact some members of the National Association of Rocketry to find out more information about piston launchers.

## Drag Force Determination

**Project**: Show how you can determine the drag on a rocket.

### Background:

The section in this book about wind tunnels and the section titled: *Coefficient of Drag Estimation from Altitude Measurements,* describes methods of determining the coefficient of drag ($C_d$) of a rocket. The second method involves tracking the model and then using computer software to find the $C_d$ of the model (the associated $C_d$ for the model to reach this altitude).

The purpose of this project is to demonstrate this process of determining the $C_d$ of the model. If you have a wind tunnel, you can also compare the two methods of measuring the $C_d$.

For this method to work, the model must fly a straight and vertical trajectory, and the ejection charge must deploy at the very top of the flight. Otherwise, the results will not be very accurate. This makes it important to choose the right rocket motor for your model.

### Where to Start:

Read the section in this book called *Coefficient of Drag Estimation from Altitude Measurements* on how to determine the drag coefficient of a model with optical tracking. Also read the section on optical tracking too.

## Drag Reduction Techniques #1

**Project**: Show that by streamlining the fins of a rocket, it will fly higher.

### Background:

The easiest method of decreasing the drag on a model is to "airfoil" the fins. This is also called *streamlining*. By sanding the fins so that they have a "teardrop" shape, the drag on the model is reduced, and it can fly a lot higher.

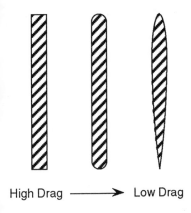

High Drag ———————→ Low Drag

In this project, you can build a variety of similar models, but the only difference being the "airfoil" shape of each fin. You might create one model with "square edge" fins, a model with rounded edge fins, and the last with fully "stream-lined" fins.

After building the models, you will fly them to see which one flies highest. When you fly them, make sure you use similar types of rocket motors and that they all weigh the same prior to lift-off. Add tracking powder to lighter models.

To avoid tracking the models, you could launch them at the same instant (with multiple pads and launch systems) and then compare them visually to see which one flew higher. If you do this, make sure you paint the models different colors so you can easily distinguish them in the air.

## Where to Start:

Read the section at the beginning of this book to find out the various methods that can be used to track your rockets to see which one flies the highest.

**Rocket Demo**

**17**

## Drag Reduction Techniques #2

**Project**: Show that by removing the launch lug from the model, it can fly higher.

## Background:

The launch lug is used with the launch rod to guide the rocket until it is flying fast enough for the fins to become effective at keeping the model flying straight. After this point, the lug serves no useful purpose. According to some rocket experts, the launch lug on the rocket can contribute up to 1/3 the total drag of the rocket. Therefore, removing it from the model should allow it to fly significantly higher.

There are a three easy methods to stabilize the model that don't require a traditional lug glued to the side of the rocket. These are: "tower" launch pads, "pop lugs," and piston launchers. Since a

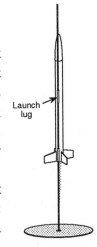

Launch lug

piston launcher will help *kick* the model into the air and can increase the overall (final) altitude, it should not be used for this demonstration.

It is a relatively easy demonstration to compare a model with a launch lug against a model without a launch lug. You fly them with the same type of rocket motor, and determine which one flew higher. Before you launch them, make sure that they both weigh the same. Add tracking powder to the light-weight model to make its mass equal to the other.

## Where to Start:

The book *Model Rocket Design & Construction* describes and shows illustrations of "pop launch lugs" and tower launch pads. Both of these are very easy to construct, so you can choose either one to conduct this demonstration.

Also read the section at the beginning of this book to find out the various methods that can be used to track your rockets to see which flies the highest.

## Drag Reduction Techniques #3

**Project:** Show that rounded nose cones have lower drag and therefore fly higher.

## Background:

This is a typical rocket project that has been performed numerous times. It demonstrates that a rounded nose cone has lower drag than a blunt nose cone shape, and therefore will allow the rocket to fly higher.

For useful data, you shouldn't try to compare more than two or three nose cones. I suggest that a flat nose, a rounded nose, and a pointed nose are the only ones used. If you try to compare noses of slightly different shapes, you will quickly find that you can't find any significant difference between the altitudes of the rockets.

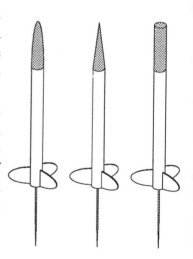

## Where to Start:

Start by reading the section in this book that tells you how to track the altitude of a rocket.

When flying your rockets, make sure that all the models weigh the same before they are launched. It may be necessary to add weight to lighter models to make them heavier. I suggest that tracking powder be used, as it is very simple to add it to an already constructed model.

For this demonstration, it would be best to use only one model for all the flights, and change the nose cone between flights. This would eliminate any effects to the final results that different fins or different construction techniques might create.

Rocket
Demo

## 19 Drag Reduction Techniques #4

**Project:** Show that by streamlining and other drag reduction methods that the model that it will fly higher.

## Background:

Reducing the drag of a model will allow it to fly higher into the air. There are many techniques that can be used that reduce the drag on a model. These include: streamlined fins, fin fillets, boat-tails, smooth painted surfaces, smaller diameter models, three fins instead of four, removal of the launch lugs, and the shape of the nose cone.

In this project, you should select and build a "typical" model, and then build a similar rocket, but with all the drag reduction techniques added. After building the models, you will fly them to see which flies highest. When you fly them, make sure you use identical types of rocket motors in each model, and that each model weighs the same before liftoff.

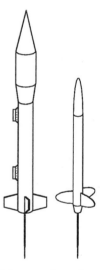

It is also possible to launch both rockets at the same time, and then just visually compare which flew the highest instead of tracking each rocket flight.

## Where to Start:

The book *Model Rocket Design & Construction* has a special section on the various drag reduction techniques that can be used on your model.

Also read the section at the beginning of this book to find out the various methods that can be used to track your rockets to see which flies the highest.

Rocket Demo

**20**

## Types of Gliders #1

**Project**: Show the various types of gliders that are used with model rockets.

## Background:

For the person who would like to demonstrate gliders with rockets, a good topic to choose is to show the many different types of gliders. Not only does this include boost gliders versus rocket gliders, but you can also demonstrate front-engine versus rear-engine gliders, and the three different wing positions that are typical for airplanes: canard configuration, conventional configuration and the tailless airplane configuration.

## Where to Start:

The book *Model Rocket Design & Construction* has a very large section about the different types of gliders used in rocketry. It is probably the best source of information you can find on this topic. It also lists the advantages and disadvantages of each configuration.

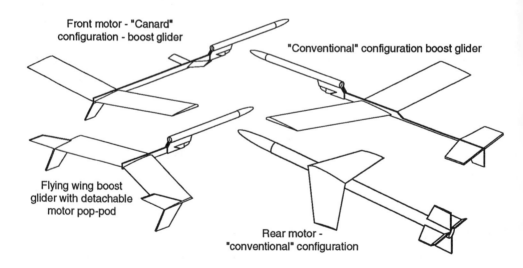

Front motor - "Canard" configuration - boost glider

"Conventional" configuration boost glider

Flying wing boost glider with detachable motor pop-pod

Rear motor - "conventional" configuration

## Types of Gliders #2

**Project**: Show the difference between fixed wing and flexible wing gliders.

### Background:

The difference between stiff fixed wings and flexible fabric wings on gliders is: the flex-wing can be folded up and inserted inside the main body tube. The main advantage of the flex wing glider is that it can be boosted higher into the air because it has a smaller frontal area — and therefore less drag.

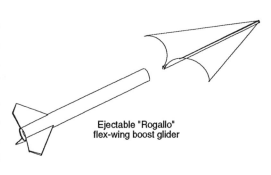

Ejectable "Rogallo" flex-wing boost glider

This demonstration would show the advantages of the flex wing glider versus fixed wing, as well as list any comparative disadvantages.

### Where to Start:

The book *Model Rocket Design & Construction* has a very large section about the different types of gliders used in rocketry. It is probably the best source of information you can find on this topic.

Plans for flex wing gliders can be obtained from the National Association of Rocketry Technical Service (NARTS). Their address is listed in Appendix A at the end of this book.

## Multi-Stage Rockets with Gliding Boosters

**Project**: Develop a booster stage that utilizes glider recovery.

### Background:

The purpose of this project is to develop a booster stage on a multi-staged rocket that utilizes glide recovery instead of tumble recovery. You could use this demonstration to find out if there is any advantage to glide recovery versus tumble recovery for booster sections.

## Where to Start:

Since there are no rocket kits currently available that use gliding boosters, you will have to make your own. Start with the book *Model Rocket Design & Construction*. It contains a section on multi-stage rockets, which gives some ideas for making a gliding booster section.

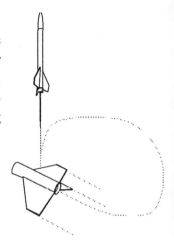

**Rocket Demo**

## 23   Rocket Finishing Techniques

**Project**: Demonstrate various finishing and painting techniques for rockets.

## Background:

The reason for creating a smooth finish on a model is twofold. First, it makes an attractive looking rocket and second, a smooth finish has less drag and will fly higher.

The purpose of this project is to develop a quick and easy method of creating a smooth surface finish

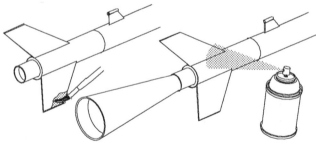

on a rocket. The finish should not only be smooth, but also be light weight and easy to create quickly.

## Where to Start:

The two biggest problem areas in creating a smooth rocket are the balsa fins, and the spirals on the body tube. It would be possible to conduct this demonstration without flying any models at all. You could just show how to make a smooth piece of balsawood and a smooth cardboard tube.

There are a variety of paints, sandpapers, primers, and fillers that can be tried.

You can start your selection process by making a visit to your local hardware store. Find out what types of products can be used for filling the grain in wood.

The book *"Model Rocket Design and Construction"* also has a section on creating a nice finish on models. You may wish to read this section to either gain starting hints, or to compare advice after you have completed your test samples.

## Optimum Mass of Rockets

**Project**: Show that there is a "best" mass for any rocket motor for achieving the highest altitude.

### Background:

There is a certain mass of a rocket that will allow the model to travel to its highest level for each different type of rocket motor. This is called the "optimum" mass for the model. A rocket that is too heavy will not fly as high as a lighter weight one. This is easy to demonstrate and is also logical to most modelers. But, if the model is too light, it will not travel to its maximum potential altitude. A good example of this is a person throwing a ping-pong ball versus a smooth golf ball. The heavier ball will travel a lot farther, even though it weighs more.

So somewhere between too heavy and too light is the "optimum" mass of the model with that particular motor.

### Where to Start:

The optimum mass for any particular motor can be found by running computer simulations to find out how heavy the model should be to fly the highest. Computer software that predicts the altitude of a model can be found from several manufacturers. Look in the latest issue of *High Power Rocketry* or *Sport Rocketry* magazines to find such manufacturers. If you can't find any, contact Apogee Components, which sells this type of software too.

When doing flight demonstrations, choose a "mini" or "micro" rocket motors. These have lower weight cases. With larger motors, the thick paper case adds a lot of weight to the model. Most of the "regular" rocket motors weigh so much, that it is nearly impossible to build a rocket around them that isn't already over the optimum mass.

Even by choosing a smaller motor, you will still have to be careful to build the model extremely light. You want to show that this model doesn't fly as high as a heavier model. You can then add weight (in the form of tracking powder) to make it heavier when flying it again.

You should also read the section in this book that describes the various tracking techniques that you can use to determine how high your rocket flies. Once you've launched and tracked the various models, you can make a graph that displays the weight of the model versus its altitude.

You can also show that the optimum mass varies if the diameter of the model is changed or if drag coefficients are different. *{see also Experiment #38.}*

Rocket Demo
**25**

## Thermal Detection Methods

**Project**: Demonstrate various methods of detecting thermals.

### Background:

Thermals are rising columns or "bubbles" of warm air. As the sun heats the ground, it warms the air above the surface. This warm air, because it becomes less dense, tends to rise. This creates the "thermal."

These thermals can affect the model rockets we fly; particularly if the models are extremely light and use large parachutes.

Sometimes it is advantageous for a model to get caught in a thermal, such as in contests, where the objective is to stay in the air for as long as possible. When a model does get caught in a

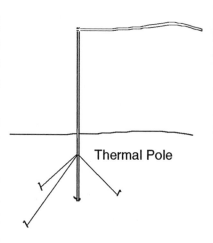

Thermal Pole

thermal, it's descent rate decreases, and in some cases, the model can rise upward. But when warm air rises, some other cooler air must descend. If your rocket gets caught in the descending air, it can fall much faster.

The intent of this project is to show that even though it is not possible to see a thermal, you can still detect its presence.

### Where to Start:

Since a thermal is caused by warm air, the first clue to detecting one is sensing a quick rise in the temperature. This can be measured with a digital thermometer. The thermometer must have a quick response time, because a thermal may pass by in only a few seconds.

Another method is to place tall poles upwind of the launch pad and attach very long, thin streamers to their tops. When a thermal passes, it will lift the streamer above the top of the pole.

A final detection method is to blow soap bubbles into the wind. When the bubbles get caught in a thermal, they will rise with the warm air. This will easily allow you to "see" where on the field the thermal is.

Using all three of these methods, you can easily detect the presence of a thermal, and devise a strategy of when to launch your rocket either to enter into it or avoid it.

Rocket
Demo

**26**

## Rocket Stability

**Project**: Demonstrate the relationship of fin size and position on the stability of a model rocket.

## Background:

Everyone knows that the fins on a model rocket are used to stabilize it in flight. Without them, the model will loop dangerously. The purpose of this project is to demonstrate that there is a minimum fin area necessary to keep the rocket flying in a stable manner.

***IMPORTANT NOTE:*** This can be a risky demonstration, because you will be making the model less stable, so it might loop around wildly. Therefore, take the precaution of flying the models in a wide open field with no spectators. Also, make sure that the grass is not dry or could easily catch on fire.

To start the project, you will build the model with rectangular shaped fins as shown in the first illustration on the next page. If it flies straight, then you will shave a little bit of wood off the tip edge — to make it shorter. After adding a little weight to the rocket to compensate for less fin mass, fly it again. By repeating this process, you will find that the model will start to wobble in flight, and eventually become completely unstable. You should stop reducing the fin area before the model flies completely unstable.

This project could be varied in two ways. First, instead of trimming wood off the fins, they could be positioned slightly forward between flights. This will also cause the model to become unstable eventually.

The second variation to the basic project is to sweep the fins aft. This will make the model slightly more stable. Because of this, you could continue to remove material from the tip edge to shorten them up more.

## Where to Start:

The book *"Model Rocket Design and Construction"* gives some basic dimensions for a typical model rocket. You can use the fin dimensions given in the book as a starting point for the first rocket flight.

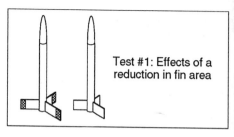

Test #1: Effects of a reduction in fin area

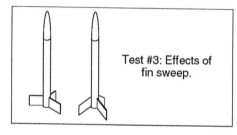

Test #2: Effects of fin placement

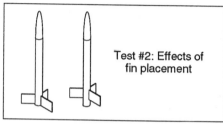

Test #3: Effects of fin sweep.

# Appendix A

# Where to get further information

There have been many other research projects involving model rocketry. Unfortunately, the results of all this research is scattered in many different places. You will not find it by looking in an encyclopedia. Your best source is talking to other modelers. So, start with your friends who are already involved in model rocketry.

If you can't find anyone that knows where to find the information you need, contact the National Association of Rocketry (N.A.R.). The N.A.R. is a national organization of modelers who may be able to direct you to someone in your area that can help you out. You can contact them by writing to: N.A.R., Box 177, Altoona, WI 54720, U.S.A. (telephone number 1-800-262-4872). The N.A.R. also sells many excellent technical reports which are available through the National Association of Rocketry Technical Service (NARTS). You can get their latest catalog by writing to: NARTS, P.O. Box 1482, Saugus, MA 01906.

You can contact other modelers directly and much faster if you have access to a computer and a modem. Many modelers 'hang-out' on computer networks, such as the "ROCKETRY" forum on the Compuserve Information Service or in the INTERNET newsgroup "rec.models.rockets". These online computer sources are actually a better source of information than the N.A.R., because they are able to answer your requests for information much faster (usually overnight).

A very good source of information is Apogee Components. As a leader in model rocket manufacturing, they have a very knowledgeable staff of people that will be able to answer your questions directly and point you in the right direction. There address is: Apogee Components, 1431 Territory Trail, Colorado Springs, CO 80919-3323 USA (web site: www.ApogeeRockets.com).

If all you need is information on building techniques, I strongly suggest the book *"Model Rocket Design & Construction"* by Timothy S. Van Milligan (ISBN 0-89024-561-4, Kalmbach Publishing Company, 1995). Not only does the book give you guidelines on constructing durable models, it also contains a glossary of more than 500 terms that will help you in case you don't understand a rocketry related word or phrase. In addition, the book has a chapter on payloads that can be flown with model rockets. Contact Apogee Components which sells this book.

# Appendix B

# Getting Free Supplies for Your Science Fair Projects

It is possible for you to obtain free supplies for your rocketry science fair experiments. If you use materials and motors from Apogee Components, you can receive a reimbursement of up to $10 worth of rocket merchandise. The supplies that are available in this program are motors, rocket kits, literature, and parts.

Please note: the free supplies are only available for experiments, and *not demonstration projects*. There are also other conditions that apply:

■ You must purchase the materials in advance directly from Apogee Components. Please save your receipts and packing slips for verification of purchase.

■ Reimbursement of supplies is with a "merchandise certificate" good only for products from Apogee Components. No cash reimbursements will be offered.

■ You will NOT be reimbursed for materials purchased from other rocket manufacturers.

■ Your merchandise certificate will be issued to you only after a *copy* of the **full** science fair project report has been received by Apogee Components.

■ Apogee Components is granted the rights to publish the "summary" results of your project.

■ Maximum value of materials for reimbursement is $10 (shipping not included).

■ Apogee Components reserves the right to disqualify any project that has been previously performed. If in doubt, check with Apogee Components first so that you will not be disappointed.

■ This promotion may be cancelled or modified at any time, and reimbursement is NOT guaranteed. Contact Apogee Components before starting your experiment to see if this offer has been modified.

■ One entry only per family.

To take advantage of this offer or for a free catalog, please contact Apogee Components at:

email: 102374.2533@compuserve.com

Apogee Components, Inc.
708 Piedra Dr., Suite C
Cañon City, CO 81212-2253
USA

# Test Your Designs Before You Fly Them!

The most important aspect of designing your own model rockets is "Safety." You need to now if it will fly straight and true so that it doesn't create a safety hazzard. The *RockSim* software has been created to allow you to check our models for stability before you launch them, and it will tell you how high they will go.

*RockSim* is a full-featured "design & simulation" software. As you design your model, it is calculating the mass, as well as the CG location so it can determine *static* stability. *RockSim* can also predict the trajectory of your rocket in any wind and at any launch angle. This is part of the *dynamic* stability check the software performs.

*RockSim* allows "any" shape fin planform, so you can really design great-looking rockets. The CAD-like features of the fin shape editor make it easy to design fins. Just click on the grid to add a corner point, and drag them around to the shape you want. There also a precision radius tool to create rounded edges. It even wraps the fin's root edge to a curved boattail!

The graphs created by the program are really awesome, and they will greatly enhance the appearance of our science fair project, because they are very accurate and easy to read. Plus, you can export data to other preadsheet programs, so that the data can be further manipulated!

*RockSim* is used by the most rocket manufacturers to confirm their designs. You should too!

The Apogee Components web site contains a ***FREE demo version*** of the software that you can download and install on your computer (Win95 or Win98 is required). The web site is: www.apogeerockets.com.

## Some of the many features of RockSim

- The only program with prediction of Dynamic Stability and wind-modified trajectory!
- Three methods of "Static CP" calulation: Barrowman, Cardboard Cut-out, "Fossey/RockSim."
- Center-of-Gravity estimation and static stability is analyzed as you design!
- Altitude prediction using 4th order Runge-Kutta iterations, or the faster Euler methods.
- Coefficient-of-Drag prediction: with transonic and supersonic effects.
- $C_d$ is broken down into components like: fin drag, profile drag, etc.
- $C_d$ is also modified as the model changes angle of attack because of wind.
- Optimum mass prediction: Malewicki plots showing altitude vs. mass.
- Design any size rocket: Massive database of parts included!
- Add your own materials and components to the databases.
- Expanded database of rocket motors now included with the program.
- Create or modify motor thrust curves (rasp.eng files): to increase accuracy.
- Graph out simulation results like: velocity, altitude, thrust, drag, etc.
- Export the raw graph data to other spread sheet programs for even more manipulation of data.
- Print graphs, parts lists, pattern sheets, and performance summaries.
- Supports 3 stages: simulates delayed staging & boosted darts too.
- Cluster motors (up to 6): mixed motors & airstarts in cluster is allowed.
- Determine parachute & streamer sizes using the descent rate calculator.
- New nose & tail cones: Von Karman, Sears-Haack, Elliptical, Power Series, and Parabolic Series.
- Change any of the measurement units to make it comfortable for you!
- Easy-to-learn interface with online "help manual."
- Sample rocket designs included to help you see how it works.
- Share your designs with other models by using the RockSim Design Library on the Apogee Components web site. Study their designs too!

# Other Great Products From Apogee Components!

## Model Rocket Propulsion
Product No. 1002
$9.95 plus $2.50 S&H

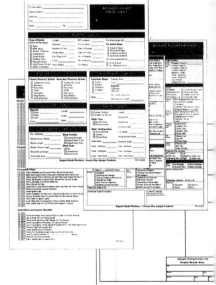

This two-volume publication explains in simple terms how a model rocket motor works. Through many hands-on demonstrations, you'll understand the basic principles of rocketry, and how model rocket motors are similar to the solid rockets used by the Space Shuttle to launch astronauts into orbit. By knowing how a rocket motor operates, you will understand *why* they are used by NASA to explore space.

Because it is written in a textbook format, this book can be used as the foundation for an educational unit on rocketry or space exploration. And besides having ton of illustrations to explain the text, most chapters also contain example questions to test th knowledge gained by the reader or student.

11 easy to understand chapters: A Brief History of the Rocket, Newton's Laws of Motior Momentum and Newton's Second Law of Motion, The Thrust Equation, The Operation of th Model Rocket Motor, Model Rocket Motor Classification, Specific Impulse - A measure of rocket's efficiency, Rocket Motor Examples, Basic Rocket Performance, Multi-Stage Rocket and Clustered Engine Rockets.

The second, 12 page booklet describes more than 16 different rocket demonstrations that can b performed to provide "hands-on" learning of the basic rocket principles. Also included is a fu answer key to all the questions in the main text. Recommended for grades 6 and above.

## Rocket Data Sheet Collection
Product No. 35509
$3.75 plus $1.50 S&H

The rocket data sheets described in the text of *69 Simple Science Fair Projects with Model Rockets* are available together at a huge discount! You can now start you Project Logbook with these professional forms for the low price of $3.75. This is 50¢ off the regular price of the individual forms.

*Send payment to:*
  *Apogee Components, Inc.*
  *1431 Territory Trail*
  *Colorado Springs, CO 80919-3323*
  *USA*